MATCHLESS AJS MOTORCYCLES

CW00822358

DRUG STORE   PRICES Photographic SERVICE.

COUGH LINCTUS 2

NO PARKING

MATCHLESS MOTOR CYCLES LTD 44

44 H. COLLIER & SONS Ltd 44

The story of one man's apprenticeship & working life in the AMC factory, Plumstead, London

Motorcycle
Apprentice

Matchless
– in name and reputation

VELOCE PUBLISHING

Other great books from Veloce –

Speedpro Series
4-cylinder Engine – How To Blueprint & Build A Short Block For High Performance (Hammill)
Alfa Romeo DOHC High-performance Manual (Kartalamakis)
Alfa Romeo V6 Engine High-performance Manual (Kartalamakis)
BMC 998cc A-series Engine – How To Power Tune (Hammill)
1275cc A-series High-performance Manual (Hammill)
Camshafts – How To Choose & Time Them For Maximum Power (Hammill)
Competition Car Datalogging Manual, The (Templeman)
Cylinder Heads – How To Build, Modify & Power Tune Updated & Revised Edition (Burgess & Gollan)
Distributor-type Ignition Systems – How To Build & Power Tune (Hammill)
Fast Road Car – How To Plan And Build Revised & Updated Colour New Edition (Stapleton)
Ford SOHC 'Pinto' & Sierra Cosworth DOHC Engines – How To Power Tune Updated & Enlarged Edition (Hammill)
Ford V8 – How To Power Tune Small Block Engines (Hammill)
Harley-Davidson Evolution Engines – How To Build & Power Tune (Hammill)
Holley Carburetors – How To Build & Power Tune Revised & Updated Edition (Hammill)
Jaguar XK Engines – How To Power Tune Revised & Updated Colour Edition (Hammill)
MG Midget & Austin-Healey Sprite – How To Power Tune Updated & Revised Edition (Stapleton)
MGB 4-cylinder Engine – How To Power Tune (Burgess)
MGB V8 Power – How To Give Your, Third Colour Edition (Williams)
MGB, MGC & MGB V8 – How To Improve (Williams)
Mini Engines – How To Power Tune On A Small Budget Colour Edition (Hammill)
Motorcycle-engined Racing Car – How To Build (Pashley)
Motorsport – Getting Started in (Collins)
Nitrous Oxide High-performance Manual, The (Langfield)
Rover V8 Engines – How To Power Tune (Hammill)
Sportscar/kitcar Suspension & Brakes – How To Build & Modify Revised & Enlarged third Edition (Hammill)
SU Carburettor High-performance Manual (Hammill)
Suzuki 4x4 – How To Modify For Serious Off-road Action (Richardson)
Tiger Avon Sportscar – How To Build Your Own Updated & Revised 2nd Edition (Dudley)
TR2, 3 & TR4 – How To Improve (Williams)
TR5, 250 & TR6 – How To Improve (Williams)
TR7 & TR8 – How To Improve (Williams)
V8 Engine – How To Build A Short Block For High Performance (Hammill)
Volkswagen Beetle Suspension, Brakes & Chassis – How To Modify For High Performance (Hale)
Volkswagen Bus Suspension, Brakes & Chassis – How To Modify For High Performance (Hale)
Weber DCOE, & Dellorto DHLA Carburetors – How To Build & Power Tune 3rd Edition (Hammill)

Those Were The Days ... Series
Alpine Trials & Rallies 1910-1973 (Pfundner)
Austerity Motoring (Bobbitt)
Brighton National Speed Trials (Gardiner)
British Police Cars (Walker)
British Woodies (Peck)
Dune Buggy Phenomenon (Hale)
Dune Buggy Phenomenon Volume 2 (Hale)
Hot Rod & Stock Car Racing in Britain In The 1980s (Neil)
MG's Abingdon Factory (Moylan)
Motor Racing At Brands Hatch In The Seventies (Parker)
Motor Racing At Crystal Palace (Collins)
Motor Racing At Goodwood In The Sixties (Gardiner)
Motor Racing At Nassau In The 1950s & 1960s (O'Neil)
Motor Racing At Oulton Park In The 1960s (Mcfadyen)
Motor Racing At Oulton Park In The 1970s (Mcfadyen)
Three Wheelers (Bobbitt)

Enthusiast's Restoration Manual Series
Citroën 2CV, How To Restore (Porter)
Classic Car Bodywork, How To Restore (Thaddeus)
Classic Car Electrics (Thaddeus)
Classic Cars, How To Paint (Thaddeus)
Reliant Regal, How To Restore (Payne)
Triumph TR2/3/3A, How To Restore (Williams)
Triumph TR4/4A, How To Restore (Williams)
Triumph TR5/250 & 6, How To Restore (Williams)
Triumph TR7/8, How To Restore (Williams)
Volkswagen Beetle, How To Restore (Tyler)
VW Bay Window Bus (Paxton)
Yamaha FS1-E, How To Restore (Watts)

Essential Buyer's Guide Series
Alfa GT (Booker)
Alfa Romeo Spider Giulia (Booker & Talbott)
BMW GS (Henshaw)
BSA Bantam (Henshaw)
BSA Twins (Henshaw)
Citroën 2CV (Paxton)
Citroën ID & DS (Heilig)
Fiat 500 & 600 (Bobbitt)
Jaguar E-type 3.8 & 4.2-litre (Crespin)
Jaguar E-type V12 5.3-litre (Crespin)
Jaguar/Daimler XJ6, XJ12 & Sovereign (Crespin)
Jaguar XJ-S (Crespin)
MGB & MGB GT (Williams)
Mercedes-Benz 280SL-560DSL Roadsters (Bass)
Mercedes-Benz 'Pagoda' 230SL, 250SL & 280SL Roadsters & Coupés (Bass)
Morris Minor & 1000 (Newell)
Porsche 928 (Hemmings)
Rolls-Royce Silver Shadow & Bentley T-Series (Bobbitt)
Subaru Impreza (Hobbs)
Triumph Bonneville (Henshaw)
Triumph TR6 (Williams)
VW Beetle (Cservenka & Copping)
VW Bus (Cservenka & Copping)

Auto-Graphics Series
Fiat-based Abarths (Sparrow)
Jaguar MKI & II Saloons (Sparrow)
Lambretta Li Series Scooters (Sparrow)

Rally Giants Series
Audi Quattro (Robson)
Austin Healey 100-6 & 3000 (Robson)
Fiat 131 Abarth (Robson)
Ford Escort MkI (Robson)
Ford Escort RS Cosworth & World Rally Car (Robson)
Ford Escort RS1800 (Robson)
Lancia Stratos (Robson)
Peugeot 205 T16 (Robson)
Subaru Impreza (Robson)

General
1½-litre GP Racing 1961-1965 (Whitelock)
AC Two-litre Saloons & Buckland Sportscars (Archibald)
Alfa Romeo Giulia Coupé GT & GTA (Tipler)
Alfa Romeo Montreal – The Essential Companion (Taylor)
Alfa Tipo 33 (McDonough & Collins)
Alpine & Renault – The Development Of The Revolutionary Turbo F1 Car 1968 to 1979 (Smith)
Anatomy Of The Works Minis (Moylan)
Armstrong-Siddeley (Smith)
Autodrome (Collins & Ireland)
Automotive A-Z, Lane's Dictionary Of Automotive Terms (Lane)
Automotive Mascots (Kay & Springate)
Bahamas Speed Weeks, The (O'Neil)
Bentley Continental, Corniche And Azure (Bennett)
Bentley MkVI, Rolls-Royce Silver Wraith, Dawn & Cloud/Bentley R & S-Series (Nutland)
BMC Competitions Department Secrets (Turner, Chambers Browning)
BMW 5-Series (Cranswick)
BMW Z-Cars (Taylor)
Britains Farm Model Balers & Combines 1967 to 2007 (Pullen)
British 250cc Racing Motorcycles (Pereira)
British Cars, The Complete Catalogue Of, 1895-1975 (Culshaw & Horrobin)
BRM – A Mechanic's Tale (Salmon)
BRM V16 (Ludvigsen)
BSA Bantam Bible, The (Henshaw)
Bugatti Type 40 (Price)
Bugatti 46/50 Updated Edition (Price & Arbey)
Bugatti T44 & T49 (Price & Arbey)
Bugatti 57 2nd Edition (Price)
Caravans, The Illustrated History 1919-1959 (Jenkinson)
Caravans, The Illustrated History From 1960 (Jenkinson)
Carrera Panamericana, La (Tipler)
Chrysler 300 – America's Most Powerful Car 2nd Edition (Ackerson)
Chrysler PT Cruiser (Ackerson)
Citroën DS (Bobbitt)
Cliff Allison – From The Fells To Ferrari (Gauld)
Cobra – The Real Thing! (Legate)
Cortina – Ford's Bestseller (Robson)
Coventry Climax Racing Engines (Hammill)
Daimler SP250 New Edition (Long)
Datsun Fairlady Roadster To 280ZX – The Z-Car Story (Long)
Dino – The V6 Ferrari (Long)
Dodge Charger – Enduring Thunder (Ackerson)
Dodge Dynamite! (Grist)
Donington (Boddy)
Draw & Paint Cars – How To (Gardiner)
Drive On The Wild Side, A – 20 Extreme Driving Adventures From Around The World (Weaver)
Ducati 750 Bible, The (Falloon)
Ducati 860, 900 And Mille Bible, The (Falloon)
Dune Buggy, Building A – The Essential Manual (Shakespeare)
Dune Buggy Files (Hale)
Dune Buggy Handbook (Hale)
Edward Turner: The Man Behind The Motorcycles (Clew)
Fiat & Abarth 124 Spider & Coupé (Tipler)
Fiat & Abarth 500 & 600 2nd Edition (Bobbitt)
Fiats, Great Small (Ward)
Fine Art Of The Motorcycle Engine, The (Peirce)
Ford F100/F150 Pick-up 1948-1996 (Ackerson)
Ford F150 Pick-up 1997-2005 (Ackerson)
Ford GT – Then, And Now (Streather)
Ford GT40 (Legate)
Ford In Miniature (Olson)
Ford Model Y (Roberts)
Ford Thunderbird From 1954, The Book Of The (Long)
Forza Minardi! (Vigar)
Funky Mopeds (Skelton)
Gentleman Jack (Gauld)
GM In Miniature (Olson)
GT – The World's Best GT Cars 1953-73 (Dawson)
Hillclimbing & Sprinting – The Essential Manual (Short & Wilkinson)
Honda NSX (Long)
Jaguar, The Rise Of (Price)
Jaguar XJ-S (Long)
Jeep CJ (Ackerson)
Jeep Wrangler (Ackerson)
Karmann-Ghia Coupé & Convertible (Bobbitt)
Lamborghini Miura Bible, The (Sackey)
Lambretta Bible, The (Davies)
Lancia 037 (Collins)
Lancia Delta HF Integrale (Blaettel & Wagner)
Land Rover, The Half-ton Military (Cook)
Laverda Twins & Triples Bible 1968-1986 (Falloon)
Lea-Francis Story, The (Price)
Lexus Story, The (Long)
little book of smart, the (Jackson)
Lola – The Illustrated History (1957-1977) (Starkey)
Lola – All The Sports Racing & Single-seater Racing Cars 1978-1997 (Starkey)
Lola T70 – The Racing History & Individual Chassis Record 4th Edition (Starkey)
Lotus 49 (Oliver)
Marketingmobiles, The Wonderful Wacky World Of (Hale)
Mazda MX-5/Miata 1.6 Enthusiast's Workshop Manual (Grainger & Shoemark)
Mazda MX-5/Miata 1.8 Enthusiast's Workshop Manual (Grainger & Shoemark)
Mazda MX-5 Miata: The Book Of The World's Favourite Sportscar (Long)
Mazda MX-5 Miata Roadster (Long)
MGA (Price Williams)
MGB & MGB GT– Expert Guide (Auto-doc Series) (Williams)
MGB Electrical Systems (Astley)
Micro Caravans (Jenkinson)
Micro Trucks (Mort)
Microcars At Large! (Quellin)
Mini Cooper – The Real Thing! (Tipler)
Mitsubishi Lancer Evo, The Road Car & WRC Story (Long)
Montlhéry, The Story Of The Paris Autodrome (Boddy)
Morgan Maverick (Lawrence)
Morris Minor, 60 Years On The Road (Newell)
Moto Guzzi Sport & Le Mans Bible (Falloon)
Motor Movies – The Posters! (Veysey)
Motor Racing – Reflections Of A Lost Era (Carter)
Motorcycle Apprentice (Cakebread)
Motorcycle Road & Racing Chassis Designs (Noakes)
Motorhomes, The Illustrated History (Jenkinson)
Motorsport In colour, 1950s (Wainwright)
Nissan 300ZX & 350Z – The Z-Car Story (Long)
Off-Road Giants! – Heroes of 1960s Motorcycle Sport (Westlake)
Pass The Theory And Practical Driving Tests (Gibson & Hoole)
Peking To Paris 2007 (Young)
Plastic Toy Cars Of The 1950s & 1960s (Ralston)
Pontiac Firebird (Cranswick)
Porsche Boxster (Long)
Porsche 964, 993 & 996 Data Plate Code Breaker (Streather)
Porsche 356 (2nd Edition) (Long)
Porsche 911 Carrera – The Last Of The Evolution (Corlett)
Porsche 911R, RS & RSR, 4th Edition (Starkey)
Porsche 911 – The Definitive History 1963-1971 (Long)
Porsche 911 – The Definitive History 1971-1977 (Long)
Porsche 911 – The Definitive History 1977-1987 (Long)
Porsche 911 – The Definitive History 1987-1997 (Long)
Porsche 911 – The Definitive History 1997-2004 (Long)
Porsche 911SC 'Super Carrera' – The Essential Companion (Streather)
Porsche 914 & 914-6: The Definitive History Of The Road & Competition Cars (Long)
Porsche 924 (Long)
Porsche 944 (Long)
Porsche 993 'King Of Porsche' – The Essential Companion (Streather)
Porsche 996 'Supreme Porsche' – The Essential Companion (Streather)
Porsche Racing Cars – 1953 To 1975 (Long)
Porsche Racing Cars – 1976 On (Long)
Porsche – The Rally Story (Meredith)
Porsche: Three Generations Of Genius (Meredith)
RAC Rally Action! (Gardiner)
Rallye Sport Fords: The Inside Story (Moreton)
Redman, Jim – 6 Times World Motorcycle Champion: The Autobiography (Redman)
Rolls-Royce Silver Shadow/Bentley T Series Corniche & Camargue Revised & Enlarged Edition (Bobbitt)
Rolls-Royce Silver Spirit, Silver Spur & Bentley Mulsanne 2nd Edition (Bobbitt)
RX-7 – Mazda's Rotary Engine Sportscar (Updated & Revised New Edition) (Long)
Scooters & Microcars, The A-Z Of Popular (Dan)
Scooter Lifestyle (Grainger)
Singer Story: Cars, Commercial Vehicles, Bicycles & Motorcycle (Atkinson)
SM – Citroën's Maserati-engined Supercar (Long & Claverol)
Subaru Impreza: The Road Car And WRC Story (Long)
Supercar, How To Build your own (Thompson)
Taxi! The Story Of The 'London' Taxicab (Bobbitt)
Tinplate Toy Cars Of The 1950s & 1960s (Ralston)
Toyota Celica & Supra, The Book Of Toyota's Sports Coupés (Long)
Toyota MR2 Coupés & Spyders (Long)
Triumph Motorcycles & The Meriden Factory (Hancox)
Triumph Speed Twin & Thunderbird Bible (Woolridge)
Triumph Tiger Cub Bible (Estall)
Triumph Trophy Bible (Woolridge)
Triumph TR6 (Kimberley)
Unraced (Collins)
Velocette Motorcycles – MSS To Thruxton Updated & Revised (Burris)
Virgil Exner – Visioneer: The Official Biography Of Virgil M Exner Designer Extraordinaire (Grist)
Volkswagen Bus Book, The (Bobbitt)
Volkswagen Bus Or Van To Camper, How To Convert (Porter)
Volkswagens Of The World (Glen)
VW Beetle Cabriolet (Bobbitt)
VW Beetle – The Car Of The 20th Century (Copping)
VW Bus – 40 Years Of Splitties, Bays & Wedges (Copping)
VW Bus Book, The (Bobbitt)
VW Golf: Five Generations Of Fun (Copping & Cservenka)
VW – The Air-cooled Era (Copping)
VW T5 Camper Conversion Manual (Porter)
VW Campers (Copping)
Works Minis, The Last (Purves & Brenchley)
Works Rally Mechanic (Moylan)

www.veloce.co.uk

First published in October 2008 by Veloce Publishing Limited, 33 Trinity Street, Dorchester DT1 1TT, England. Fax 01305 268864/e-mail info@veloce.co.uk/web www.veloce.co.uk or www.velocebooks.com.
ISBN: 978-1-84584-179-9/UPC: 6-368470-4179-3

© Bill Cakebread and Veloce Publishing 2008. All rights reserved. With the exception of quoting brief passages for the purpose of review, no part of this publication may be recorded, reproduced or transmitted by any means, including photocopying, without the written permission of Veloce Publishing Ltd. Throughout this book logos, model names and designations, etc, have been used for the purposes of identification, illustration and decoration. Such names are the property of the trademark holder as this is not an official publication.

Readers with ideas for automotive books, or books on other transport or related hobby subjects, are invited to write to the editorial director of Veloce Publishing at the above address.
British Library Cataloguing in Publication Data - A catalogue record for this book is available from the British Library. Typesetting, design and page make-up all by Veloce Publishing Ltd on Apple Mac.Printed in India by Replika Press.

The story of one man's apprenticeship & working life in the AMC factory, Plumstead, London

Motorcycle
Apprentice

Matchless
– in name and reputation

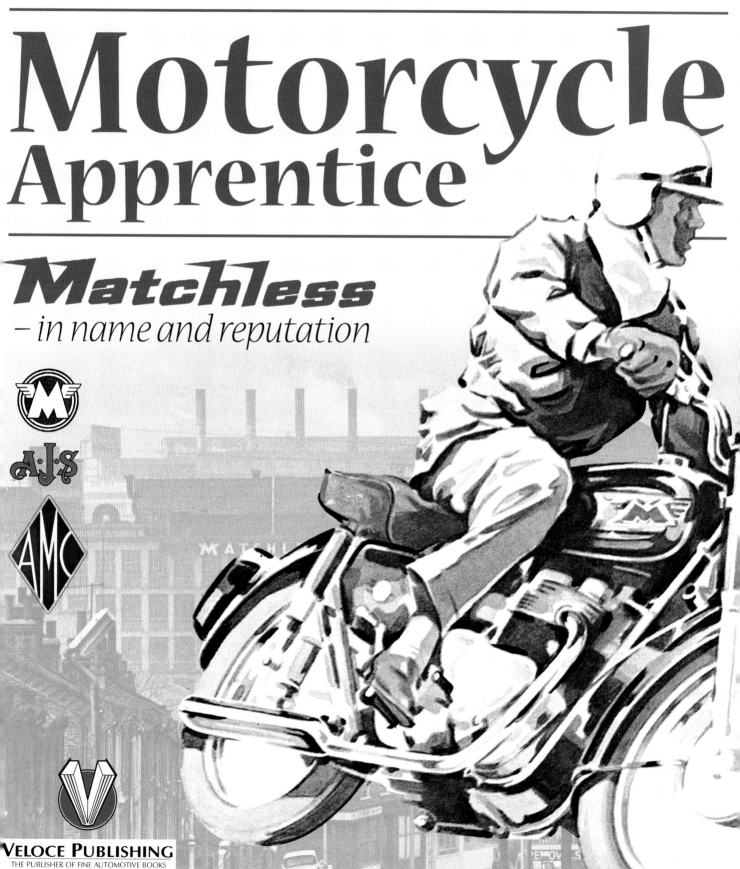

VELOCE PUBLISHING
THE PUBLISHER OF FINE AUTOMOTIVE BOOKS

Contents

This book is dedicated to all who pass their skills on to others.

Introduction

There are two reasons why this book has been written: the first is that whenever a group of like-minded motor or motorcycling enthusiasts are gathered around, stories of the past are often repeated. For many years on such occasions, friends and associates have been prompting me to record some of these experiences from an era that has now passed. For longer than I can remember, I ignored their suggestions, but, at the Homecoming Rally in Woolwich in 1989, the reality dawned on me. Nothing was the same. The factory had gone, and so, sadly, had many of the past employees. Apprenticeship training as we had known it was also a thing of the past, and if it was not soon recorded, the recollections of that era would surely fade. I was probably not the best-equipped person to make such a record, and it would be of necessity a very personal account of life at that time, but I started to make notes for my own record only. The fact that it finally turned into a book for publication is entirely due to the inspiration of one person, David Carpenter, a close friend of fellow ex-apprentice, Bernard Copleston. David had published a book about his own experiences as an apprentice in the London Docks, and it was reading this book that inspired in me the idea that the project was not only worthwhile, but necessary.

The second and more important reason is to provide a vehicle by which to convey my thanks and appreciation to every single person who took the time to teach me the skills that have helped me to survive throughout my working life. The most significant and useful education was gained during my apprenticeship at Associated Motor Cycles Ltd. I have not been spectacularly successful, and there are many who have come from humbler beginnings and have achieved much more. My only claim to fame is that I achieved much more than I ever thought could be possible; that I achieved anything at all is thanks to that apprenticeship.

I also owe a debt of gratitude to all of the friends and other ex-employees who donated information and photographs to assist me in the completion of this project. Many have stories to tell that are equally, if not more, interesting than my own, but it would be tedious and possibly libellous to repeat them all!

While every reasonable effort has been made to establish copyright ownership of the images within this book, which have come from many sources, it has not always been possible to do so. If we have inadvertently reproduced a picture without the copyright owner's permission, we offer our sincere apologies.

Bill Cakebread

1 The seed is sown

It was a long walk. Although it had been a familiar daily routine, this time it was difficult. The last remnants from my desk; compasses, books and pencils had been placed in the cardboard box with the leaving cards. The last goodbyes had been said. I walked the length of the office, past the drawing boards and down the stone staircase at the back to the factory. Out past the rows of silent gear-cutting machines, with their familiar heavy scent of cutting oil, through the material loading bay and, ducking to pass through the small personal door in the roller shutter, out into the daylight. One nostalgic glance was made to the left to look at the end of the Race Shop, and then across the road to the car park. It was hard to believe that my dream of a lifetime employment with AJS and Matchless was over. It was March 1966.

Back in 1950, Drake's 'Golden Hind' topped the weather vane on Deptford Town Hall at New Cross in south east London. It towered over the roof tops outside the windows of the main hall where I sat at assembly in Childeric Road primary school. The ship proudly proclaimed the maritime rather than the automotive history of the area where I'd been born, at 13 Bawtree Road in the war torn London of 1941. It was to be another 55 years before I discovered that the Storey motor car had been manufactured in nearby Pomeroy Street, but that venture was long gone before I arrived on the scene. Born into a family with little previous connection with motor vehicles, it was not an auspicious place to start a life-long devotion to the subject.

Bawtree Road is located in the narrowing apex of a triangle of railway lines between New Cross and New Cross Gate railway stations, where the main lines from the major towns on the south east coast converge as they approach the centre of London. To the north is the Surrey Docks, making the area an ideal target for any stray bombs that missed the targets that surrounded us. In spite of this, my Mother refused to leave my Father's side, and we lived there throughout the Second World War. After the war, there were many gaps where houses had once stood but our home and family had survived unscathed.

An Austin A40 parked outside number 13, soon after the house had been vacated by the family.

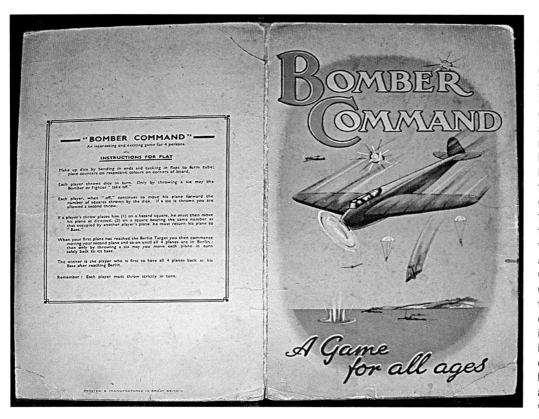

"BOMBER COMMAND"

An interesting and exciting game for 4 persons.

INSTRUCTIONS FOR PLAY

Make up dice by bending in ends and tucking in flaps to form cube; place counters on respective colours at corners of board.

Each player throws dice in turn. Only by throwing a six may the Bomber or Fighter " take off".

Each player, when "off," continues to move his plane forward the number of squares thrown by the dice. If a six is thrown you are allowed a second throw.

If a player's throw places him (1) on a hazard square, he must then move his plane as directed, (2) on a square bearing the same number as that occupied by another player's plane, he must return his plane to "Base."

When your first plane has reached the Berlin Target you then commence moving your second plane and so on until all 4 planes are in Berlin; then only by throwing a six may you move each plane in turn safely back to its base.

The winner is the player who is first to have all 4 planes back at his Base after reaching Berlin.

Remember : Each player must throw strictly in turn.

A toy from a wartime childhood; political correctness did not exist then.

The seed is sown

These gaps in the houses later provided 'playgrounds' for our childish adventures. War-games and 'Cowboys and Indians' dramas would be enacted among the scrub and gorse bushes that reclaimed the rubble, as we hid with our wooden guns behind the giant timbers that shored up the sides of the adjoining houses. A firm favourite was a site at the end of Batavia Road. It was much larger than most, and bordered the main New-Cross Road on one side. Our parents didn't like us to play there. At the time we didn't understand why, but it eventually transpired that it had once been the site of a Woolworth's store that had received a direct hit by a V2 rocket one lunchtime, when the store was packed with weekend shoppers. I am led to believe that it was the greatest loss of life caused by a single bomb prior to Hiroshima. We later learned that, apart from the devastating loss of so many lives, the reason it upset my parents so much was that after the crater had been filled in, sounds had been heard from survivors trapped in the basement. They excavated again but no further survivors were found. I am glad that in our childish innocence we were totally unaware of, and were shielded from, the true horrors that had produced our playgrounds.

I lived at number 13, in the upper flat of a two-storey terraced house, with my parents and younger brother, Robert, until I was 21. The downstairs flat was occupied by my maternal Grandparents, Alfred and

One of my Father's brothers, Arthur (left), with a downed Messerschmitt in the desert.

Mabel Parsons, and it was a happy childhood. There was no division between the two flats other than the open staircase, but this presented no difficulties in our poor but harmonious family. When we grew older and outgrew the accommodation in the upstairs flat, I moved out of the bedroom that I'd shared with my younger brother to live with my Grandparents downstairs. In truth, it was a room that was not popular. It was dark, and its door was at an unlit corner of the passageway under the stairs. It was the place where my mother had been terrified by the vision of a former navy boyfriend on the night that he went down with the 'Hood.' That historic incident itself held no personal fear for me, but the gaslit house was full of eerie shadows. Born when London was being bombed, I had grown up with an innate fear of the dark and loud noises. It was at its worst on winter nights, coming home from school first when everyone was still at work, and having the duty of lighting the gas lamps, warming the mantles gently with the match and waiting for the 'pop' as I pulled the chain to turn on the gas. Insufficient warming of the mantle, or turning on the gas too quickly, would cause the fragile mantle to explode, leaving me with a jet of useless flame and precious little light. Worse than that, it undermined my confidence to light the next one!

My Father spent the whole of his working life as a Storeman at Merryweathers in Greenwich High Road, manufacturer of fire engines. He was there when war broke out and, as the demand for fire appliances was critical, his was a reserved occupation. He always felt bitter about this, and made up for it by becoming an auxiliary fireman, one of those brave people who fought with fire pumps towed behind taxis to prevent London from burning during the blitz. In spite of this dangerous activity, he still regretted that he was not involved in the front line war effort like some of his brothers, and pictures sent back from the front did nothing to ease his frustration with his reserved occupation.

One night, later in the war, he was on fire-watch duty with another member of staff when the factory received a direct hit from a V1 'flying bomb.' Father dived under a water storage tank supported on brick piers while the walls of the factory collapsed around him. Miraculously, both of the duty fire-watchers survived; the only casualty, apart from the factory itself, being a civilian pedestrian who had been passing by at the time.

Merryweathers, flattened by the V1, keeps on working. My Father was one of two on fire watch duty that night. Incredibly, they both survived.

from his colleagues as they drove past on the trains! His allotment was laid out with precision, and kept the family (and a good many of the neighbours) supplied with fresh vegetables, and even grapes, throughout the war and long afterwards. As a child, I spent much of my weekends with him on that allotment, helping with the chores and carrying home the

My paternal Grandparents lived on the north side of Grenfell Street, Greenwich, just south of the Blackwall Tunnel. This tiny house had been home to Alf and Rhoda Cakebread, their six sons and one daughter. Standing at the back door of the house, which backed onto the Greenwich gasworks, there loomed a huge and ominous gasometer, overshadowing everything and blocking out what little light managed to filter through the infamous London smogs that were a common feature of the time. As a child, just after the war, I used to stare up at that gasometer and imagine what might have been the fate of my Grandparents had it suffered a direct hit from a German bomb. Grenfell Street was the only place that I ever saw a real street gas lighter at work, travelling from lamp to lamp, steering his bicycle with one arm, with a short ladder hooked over the other shoulder. This, together with the deliveries of bread, milk, coal and beer by horse-drawn vehicles, constitute my few memories of the age that was disappearing as I grew up.

Both of my Grandfathers were in 'steam.' Closest to me was my much-loved and jolly maternal Grandfather Alf Parsons. He was a respected train driver, and the only person in our immediate family who had any kind of a profession. During the war, he also had a reserved occupation and was employed driving ammunition trains between London and Portsmouth. He loved both his work and gardening. There being no garden but only a concrete yard where we lived, he rented a large allotment on the railway embankment to the south of New Cross Gate station. Even on his days off, he would be acknowledged by a whistle

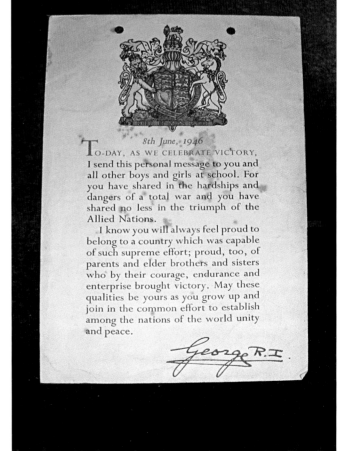

8th June, 1946

TO-DAY, AS WE CELEBRATE VICTORY, I send this personal message to you and all other boys and girls at school. For you have shared in the hardships and dangers of a total war and you have shared no less in the triumph of the Allied Nations.

I know you will always feel proud to belong to a country which was capable of such supreme effort; proud, too, of parents and elder brothers and sisters who by their courage, endurance and enterprise brought victory. May these qualities be yours as you grow up and join in the common effort to establish among the nations of the world unity and peace.

George R.I.

The King thanks me for the part that I played during the war. I would have been five years old at the time!

Motorcycle Apprentice

produce in a sack or trug basket. Never have carrots tasted so good as when pulled from that ground, rinsed in the water butt, and eaten immediately.

The journey to the allotment entailed a walk to New Cross Gate station from where we would leave the platform and walk along the track to our destination. In the summer it was lovely and on cold or wet days the journey would sometimes be livened by hitching a lift on the footplate of a shunting engine working in the sidings, where the warmth from the fire-box would be most welcome. Some of the lines were electrified and Grandfather would encourage me to step very high over the live rails when we crossed the lines. I didn't need any encouragement! He was short and wore a long rubberized coat in the winter. He claimed that he could sometimes fee l a tingle up his back as the coat tails dragged over the live rail when it was raining. Again, I had no inclination to put it to the test.

Sometimes, I would have to complete the journey home through the last few streets alone, while Grandfather visited his local pub to trade some of his produce for a well earned beer or three. My mischievous recollection of Sunday lunchtimes was to listen for Grandmother's reaction from downstairs as he habitually tumbled through the front door, late as usual, and far too cheerful for his own good. After lunch, it was a source of amusement to watch him

Grandfather Parsons doing the work that he loved.

sleep off his excesses in his favourite chair by the black-leaded range, his lit pipe slowly rotating, as his mouth relaxed, until it set fire to his shirt and woke him with a start. Grandfather had a great many burns on his shirts!

Grandfather Cakebread.

Because of the nature of his work, his hands were as tough as leather. Another of his weekly rituals that I helped him with was the refilling of his petrol lighters, and replacing worn flints ready for the working week ahead. He couldn't live without his pipe. He never used lighter fuel as that was expensive but instead used ordinary petrol from a can. It burnt black and smoky but he didn't seem to care. Spillage was inevitable and at the end of the exercise his hands would be soaked in petrol. His party trick, intended to frighten me (successfully, I might add), was to then light a match and set fire to his hands! After his audience of small children had been suitably terrified, he would simply clap out the flames and laugh. Not to be recommended. His ruddy face always smiling, he was popular and ever helpful. I loved him.

Our paternal Grandfather, Alf Cakebread, was an entirely different matter. He was more remote and only seen when the family made occasional weekend visits to his home by the Blackwall Tunnel. His seven offspring must have been keen to escape the confines of that overcrowded house because, when old enough, they all went their separate ways, and seemed to meet only by accident on rare visits to see their parents. My first memories of Alf were at the end of his working life when he was a stoker on Thames tugboats. He had spent his formative years, however, at sea on the last of the square rigged sailing ships, and this harsh upbringing showed. He had apparently been a hard father, fond of his drink, who was not afraid to use his belt to exercise his authority in the household. He was a much harder man and, therefore, for a child at least, more difficult to know. He did have his lighter side and had been an accomplished entertainer. He was very proficient on his banjo and, light on his feet, an expert step-dancer. To me, however, this tough man, swearing freely from his rocking chair by the fireside, was a bit frightening. I wish now that I'd been old enough to have understood him better.

Many stories of their harsh upbringing were told by Grandfather's siblings, repeated often enough from different sources to guarantee their accuracy. Only the sister slept in the bedroom of her parents. The six boys shared a double bed, and slept head to tail alternately like sardines in a can. The bed had one side against the wall in the small bedroom and this hiding place provided refuge from their father's bursts of anger. He was unable to reach right over to the wall and so would take off his belt and swing it wildly under the bed, buckle end flying, in the hope of striking his target. One Christmas, when the boys were fighting over a new train set bought jointly for them, the argument was settled swiftly by the train being crushed by his boot! Retribution was harsh in the Cakebread household. Discipline was all.

Apart from my Father's experiment with solo motorcycling before the war, no-one on either side of the family had ever ridden or driven anything other than a bicycle, so there was

A camping trip with the Coventry Eagle.

little precedent for the career path that I was to follow. I've often read, with some envy, the experiences of members of the current generation who have been born into families where motorized transport was the normal way of life for their parents and sometimes even their Grandparents! Like the continent's relationship with England in the early days of motoring, they had a headstart on me. If I had followed in the footsteps of my family heritage, it would have been logical that I should either have gone to sea or have been a steam enthusiast. Perhaps a steam launch on the Thames would have been more appropriate than cars and motorcycles as a career and hobby? One thing that I have certainly inherited, however, is an enduring love of the sea.

It was my Father who had been the first in the family to break the mould with a brief flirtation with solo motorcycling in the mid-1930s. This had taken the form of a pressed-steel framed Coventry Eagle motorcycle (JJ 9421) of 150cc (9.15 cubic inch) on which he had enjoyed camping holidays. On this motorized transport he had apparently wooed my Mother, and impressed her parents with his white gauntlets and apparent wealth! My Mother always said that it was the white gauntlets that had impressed them most.

Dad never really enjoyed solo motorcycling, however, and by the time that I was born, the Coventry Eagle was long gone, and

his Rudge Whitworth bicycle had become his prized possession and only form of transport. This steed gave me my first experience of handlebars and a taste for speed. From primary school, I would sometimes be transported home on a small plywood saddle that Dad had fitted to the crossbar just behind the change lever for the Sturmey-Archer hub gear. The handlebars were strange on the Rudge, being of the 'semi-dropped' pattern. The handgrips were on the outer and lower sections, while the rod brakes were operated by short, straight crossed levers, like scissors, near the stem. The brake levers were, therefore, a long way out of reach when travelling at speed! Dad's normal casual riding style was to ride with his hands close together over the brakes, but with me on board, this was where my hands rested. I was in severe danger of having my fingers crushed in the event of emergency braking! The fun part was that I was eventually trusted with operating the brakes on instruction and when I became proficient at that, with changing the gears as well. I can still remember the squeal and judder of those brakes and the whine of the dynamo lighting on the rear tyre on winter evenings.

Then the serious addiction began. I must have been about eight or nine years old when excitement came to our home in an assortment of mysterious dirty cardboard boxes. My parents said that it was going to be our very own motorbike and sidecar. At the

Early dreams. My brother and I try the Carter's Norman two-stroke for size before we were old enough to ride.

time it seemed incredulous to me that this heap of apparent junk would eventually turn into something like the gleaming Brough Superior SS100 and single seat sidecar that was owned by a person who lived on the corner of our street. I suppose that in some respects at least, I was right.

The round-topped air-raid shelter that had served as a temporary shed at the bottom of the garden (in reality, it was a concrete yard) had been demolished by the council, and in its place my Father had built a shed out of literally dozens of the wooden bunks that the shelters had housed. These had been disposed of by the local council after the war from the Ludwick Road Mission Hall, next door to the house where the Brough Superior lived. The boxes of bits were stored in this shed and, over the months that followed, I watched and learned about the

magical world of pistons, valves and cams as the motorcycle slowly took shape. When not in the shed, I read every motorcycle magazine that I could find, and unravelled the mysteries of the two- and four-stroke cycles by reading Dad's copies of *The Motorcycling Manual* and *The Motorcyclist's Workshop*. My Father had received no formal training of any kind during his life, and was learning in much the same way.

Eventually, what emerged, chrysalis-like, from the boxes was not a gleaming, nickel-plated Brough Superior, but GM 1422, a 1929 600cc Panther, hand-painted black with a distinctive maroon petrol tank adorned with two leaping tiger (Esso?) transfers on the side. When it actually fired for the first time it was a moment of elation and shock for us all, especially for our neighbours!

The Panther was, however, still a solo and there were four

Motorcycle Apprentice

of us, the fourth being my brother, Bob, five years my junior. A sidecar was needed. As I have indicated, my Father was self-taught in everything and seemed to be proficient in the use of all manner of tools. Thus, the design and building of a sidecar presented little difficulty. Expense in this instance was not an obstacle, as his employer, Merryweathers, was a manufacturer of the most beautiful coach-built and coach-painted fire-engines. Off-cuts of the best quality ash and aluminium panelling were, therefore, readily available for the asking (I am assuming that he asked!). Somewhere to build it presented a bigger problem, however, and there must have been some high level and difficult marital negotiations before it was finally constructed in the 'front room' of our first floor flat. These days, we would call it a lounge, but back then it was a cold room, too expensive to heat, and rarely used for most of the year. It housed the best furniture and the wind-up HMV gramophone, and was only used at Christmas or similar special occasions. The sidecar was eventually united with the bike by delivering it through the widow and lowering it to the street below (the widow frame had to be removed for this exercise).

It's true that what finally emerged was hardly the Brough Superior that I had dreamed of, but we were proud of it just the same. There was another hurdle to cross before we could venture forth on the road, however: the small matter of being able to ride it! During the impoverished war years, my Father had allowed his original driving licence to expire. This had been obtained before the introduction of the driving test, and a new test, therefore, had to be taken. The fact that my Father had never ridden a motorcycle combination before was a minor detail. Eventually, with the assistance of an old packing case filled with bricks lashed to the bare sidecar chassis, the necessary experience was gained and the test was passed. Over these months, I dreamed of motorcycles and nothing else. I gathered catalogues of 'affordable' two-stroke starter motorcycles for myself to ride and left them idly open at the appropriate page on my bed in the hope that my parents would buy me one. Blissfully unaware of the true state of our family finances, and my Mother's superb husbandry of them, I might as well have been asking for the moon.

Our family's venture into motorized transport is a supreme example of what can be achieved with less than nothing, if one has the will to work and the dedication to achieve; an early lesson in life that was to serve me well. The sidecar outfit was finished, but there was still precious little money available for weekend jaunts 'en famille.' To resolve this, my father used a cunning plan by which he could obtain petrol freely whilst still maintaining a clear conscience. One of his duties as Storeman was to refuel the various company vehicles and the new fire-engines before dispatch. When each vehicle was filled, he would hold the delivery nozzle as high as possible, replace the cap and then allow the small drop of fuel in the pipe to drain into a quart (1.14-litre)

oilcan by the pump. When full, the can would be brought home in the saddlebag of the trusty Rudge bicycle and eventually there would be sufficient fuel for a weekend ride to as far as Eltham, which was virtually in the Kent countryside in those days. Our time for travel and adventure had arrived!

That Panther introduced our family to a whole new world, regular journeys to the countryside and visits to family and friends that had not previously been possible. For me personally, it introduced a world of speed, excitement, and the gorgeous bark of a big single. Invariably inadequately dressed, I always tried to ride pillion behind my Father in preference to the relative comfort of the sidecar, although I was sometimes forced to abandon my position when my health was seriously endangered by the intense winter cold. The Panther also introduced my Father to an unusual period of forced idleness and pain. One day he forgot to retard the ignition when trying to start it and the beast literally propelled him vertically into the air when it kicked back. He always kept his knee bent after that lesson!

That bike also served to introduce me and my inquisitive young neighbourhood friends to magnetos and high tension electricity. The game was that I would hold the HT lead and then link hands with a circle of friends. The one at the other end of the circle would then hold the handlebars to provide an effective earth connection while my Father swung the kick-starter. The high voltage shock could be felt passing up one arm, across the chest and down the other as it travelled around the circle. Ignorance is bliss and we all thought that it was fun at the time. In retrospect, we should be grateful that none of us suffered from a heart problem!

My Father eventually sold that combination and bought GLY 748, a 500cc V-twin ex-War Department Indian which, in turn, was exchanged for a 600cc VB side valve Ariel (WMK 526, and our first experience of a spring frame). A succession of similar spring-heel 'Golden Flash' BSA twins followed, the first of which being WMK 555. Each purchase involved the building of yet another sidecar, as Dad slowly improved the quality of his mounts and honed his coach-building skills. My only interest was in two wheels, however, and by now I had come to realize that ownership would only come through efforts of my own.

By now, my younger brother Bob and I were both keen to emulate our Father, and become motorcyclists ourselves. Our parents had friends, the Carters, who lived at Catford, and had a son, Alan, a few years older than me. They were the only people that we knew who owned a solo motorcycle, a Norman, and their son had a small auto-cycle. We knew them as 'Uncle' and 'Aunt' and the families would holiday together, but sadly Alan was killed in a road accident at Biggin Hill one evening. Losing their only son was a terrible blow to both them and our parents and, understandably, this did nothing to encourage them to support our own motorcycling ambitions.

2 First bike

A heavy Hercules upright and rod-braked cycle had been purchased for me as a Christmas present by my parents, no doubt at great personal sacrifice. I learned to ride on it, but it was thanklessly abandoned in favour of a more sporting Raleigh with cable brakes when I moved school from Childeric Road primary to Wilson's grammar at Camberwell. It was not a happy change (the school, not the bike!). From being a star pupil at primary school, I degenerated progressively with each succeeding year in the stuffy public school atmosphere that pervaded in my secondary grammar school. By the time I had reached 16 years of age, they had destroyed any pride that I once had in academic achievement, and my thoughts were dominated by means of escape from school to earn a living of my own. My only good

The proud owner of his first motorcycle at Winchelsea Beach.

Picnic in Norfolk. School friend Dave Jackman is able to join the family travelling on the VB Ariel now that I am riding independently.

memories of that school, apart from a few close friends, were an excellent teacher of religious instruction, who we nicknamed 'Yarweh,' and the rifle range where, by joining the 'Combined Cadet Force' and pretending to be soldiers, we could use the .22 bored-down .303 Lee Enfield rifles in a fenced-off part of the playground. The RI teacher was wonderful in that he avoided specific religious dogma and gave us a good grounding and appreciation of all world religions. It was not appreciated at the time, but now I realize that more of his type in schools would be the greatest contribution to world peace that I can imagine. The only person to whom I felt any envy was an older boy, whose family clearly had money, who rode to school on a Vincent Comet!

My inspiration at this time was *The Daily Mail Motorcycling Guide-1952*, which catalogued the specifications of the current machines. The last page of the motorcycle section (the guide also covered scooters, auto-cycles, cycle-motors and three-wheelers in alphabetical order), covered the Vincent twins. What a dreamer I was! I just had to have a 'bike of my own, and to do this meant that I had to earn some money. At the age of about

13, the solution came by way of a paper round. The round was an early one, and a long one, and a bicycle was essential. The small sweet shop and tobacconist was near the canal bridge, on a bend opposite Folkestone Gardens, a lovely name given to two of four dowdy blocks of flats still standing (the other two had been bombed during the war). The shop was run by a rotund ex-policeman who kept a large truncheon beside the till in case he should encounter a difficult customer or a petty thief. There was little 'political correctness' in dealing with thieves in those days. The pay was seven shillings and sixpence per week which I saved exclusively for my motorcycle and eventually my hoard became sufficient for a deposit.

An occasional Saturday morning treat was a ride on the pillion with Dad to visit Pride and Clarke's showrooms in Stockwell Road, Brixton, and on rare occasions to travel further afield to Comerfords at Thames Ditton. I don't recall any real purpose for the visits other than escapism on my Father's part, and the rare times when we needed to trawl through the excellent breaker's department at Pride and Clarke's for some secondhand spare or other extra, like leg-shields for his combination.

One of my Father's later sidecar creations demonstrates his craftsmanship. The BSA B33 can be seen leaning against the wall in the background.

Still at school and too young to be able to ride, I cajoled my Father into regular trips to the dealers. Eventually, at Comerfords, way past all of the gleaming new bikes in the showroom, at the back of the shop was what would be best described as the 'dead park' where the cheapest trade-ins sheltered in the gloom. HDT 276 was a 1947 250cc side-valve BSA C.10. It hardly represented exciting motorcycling but, at the time, it was a dream, and the purchase price, at £17-10s, was just about affordable by paying a 33 per cent deposit, with the balance on hire purchase. The fact that there would be nothing left of my income after paying the monthly instalments didn't seem to concern me at all. It was scruffy, of course, but it was quite clean, and there was still chrome on the green panelled petrol tank. The tank was loose, and there was nothing holding the tank-mounted speedometer in place except its drive cable. The 'bike did run (the small end rattled), the gearbox functioned, and the work that was needed was within my limited abilities and non-existent budget at the time - the deal was done.

I replaced the small end bush, did a valve grind, painted the 'bike and generally made it look smart in time for my 16th birthday and my first provisional driving licence. By this time I had hoped to be in work so that I could afford those little luxuries like tax, insurance, and petrol, etc.

The waiting time was not wasted as I filled it by teaching myself the art of clutch control and gear changing by riding it

in the dirt clearing surrounded by Nissen hut garages that our house conveniently backed onto. As it turned out, I could not leave school until after the GCE exams, which meant in the spring of 1958, my 17th year. Somehow or other, I managed to earn, beg or borrow (courtesy of Grandfather Parsons, who was the only saver in the family), sufficient cash to tax and insure the bike. With many like-minded friends, it was a summer of fun and anticipation before entering the real world of work and earning one's keep. That summer, the bike was taken on a family holiday to Norfolk, enabling my best friend at school to come along with us and occupy the pillion seat on the family combination that I had vacated. The holiday did not start well for me. I was still a novice at clutch control and the cork clutch in the BSA was not the kindest in the world. I had not yet learned the art of slipping the 'box' into neutral while still moving and when, only a few miles from home, we met heavy traffic in the Blackwall Tunnel, the clutch seized and would not free. It was a long hard push out of that fume-filled tunnel, and when I finally emerged, I found the rest of my concerned family waiting. I then learned that waiting for the clutch to cool was the simple and only remedy, and that my exhaustion had all been in vain. After that, the holiday improved daily, together with my confidence, and I had added another lesson in the art of motorcycling to my meagre experience.

3 The interview

My parents had committed to my staying at Wilson's grammar school until I was 18 years of age, but my pathetic performance in the many GCE examinations that I sat in my 16th year (I passed only in English Language and Woodwork!) convinced me that there was no longer an academic future available to me. My family could ill afford to keep me there anyway, and I wanted to work. I had no idea what I might be able to do, and the only clear thought in my head was that I wanted to work with motorcycles. Eventually, end of term came around and I simply didn't go back. The school wrote a threatening letter to my parents, but I was resolute and the need for another income in the family meant that there was no resistance from my parents. The school did not pursue the matter and, bearing in mind my poor academic performance, I could understand why.

It seemed a distant hope, but with only one ambition in mind, I wrote a letter to Associated Motor Cycles Ltd. at Plumstead, the only motorcycle manufacturer within reach of my home. As a back-up, I also applied to the well respected engineering company Molins of Deptford, manufacturer of cigarette making machinery. They had a reputation for good engineering and training and were closer to home. I had absolutely no interest whatsoever in the end product but I needed to find a job – any job so that I could at least afford to keep the BSA. The paper round was just enough to pay the hire-purchase repayments, but little else. It was the Molins interview that came up first. The interview went well and I was encouraged when I heard that I had scored 98 per cent in the entrance examination. My confidence was soon to be shattered, however, when the letter arrived containing the news that I had not secured the offer of an apprenticeship. The letter explained that it was due to the very high quality of applicants that they had received, and that I had got just one answer wrong. I recall the question clearly: "What is the formula for the volume of the frustum of a cone?" The interviewer had been kind and gave me a simple suggestion

as to how the formula could be remembered in the future. It is a formula that I have never forgotten!

Subconsciously, I think that my intention was to emulate my Father by giving loyal service and devoting a lifetime career to one company. Unfortunately, the door to Merryweathers was also closed. I don't know to this day whether my Father had high principles and didn't believe in nepotism, had no faith in the training facilities at Merryweathers, or if he simply didn't want me to see how he behaved when he was away from the marital home. Judging by the lipstick stains, he was obviously popular with the office girls at Christmas! Whatever his reasons, it was clear that he had no intention of helping me to secure a job with his company and this was not an option.

All of my hopes now hung on my real dream of working at AMC which just happened to be the only other job application outstanding. After a seemingly endless wait, the offer of an interview finally arrived. I just wanted a job there, any job at all. By now I was desperate. This was what I really wanted.

Associated Motor Cycles Ltd. was, of course, unique in being the only motorcycle manufacturer located in the south of England, so there really was only one opportunity available. It is often said that there is a north/south divide in this country, with a line drawn across the country at Watford Gap. This is certainly true of the motorcycle industry, but in this case it is inverted, as few seem to think that there was ever any industry south of Watford. I have repeatedly heard it said and seen it written that Plumstead was a most unsuitable place to build a motorcycle factory, being located so far from the industrial Midlands, but this was simply not true. All along the bank of the Thames in and downstream of central London was a vast area of industry outside of the docks, the remnants of which can still be seen today. Sub-contract suppliers existed in abundance. One of the largest engineering employers, the Royal Arsenal, stood just across the road from the AMC factory, and on the other side of

The interview

the river could be seen the massive complex that was Ford's main production plant in the UK. Just a mile or two to the east was Stones of Charlton, the foundry that supplied the aluminium castings to AMC. Again, this was a company that could rival any of the capabilities offered in Birmingham or Coventry, which had cast and machined the propellers for the Queen Mary, no less! The whole area has a proud history of shipbuilding and engineering that stretches back centuries, and there is absolutely no need to apologize for the location. It was most suitable.

The invitation said that a parent must attend with the interviewee. Dad took me on the Indian combination and, on this one occasion, I dressed smartly and rode in the sidecar to keep myself tidy. We passed the front offices in Plumstead Road and parked in Maxey Road, the Indian looking very out of place

with the row of new motorcycles parked with their rear wheels against the kerb a few yards away. The sight of them and the sounds from the busy factory made me even more enthusiastic to work there. We entered through the front offices and that was probably one of only half a dozen times that I ever used that entrance during the whole of my employment. The works entrance and car parks were at the rear in Burrage Grove so, apart from office staff that used public transport, there was never a reason to use it, not even on the last day when I left!

I was nervous and found the interview very intimidating sitting in front of the selection panel, which comprised Directors and selected senior management, including Mr Coomber, the Personnel Manager. I faced them, answered their questions and hoped that my genuine enthusiasm would shine through my

The front entrance to the offices in Plumstead Road. Maxey Road is the next turning on the right just past the end of the buildings. (Courtesy Mortons)

ASSOCIATED MOTOR CYCLES LTD.
MANUFACTURERS OF A·J·S AND MATCHLESS MOTOR CYCLES

PLUMSTEAD ROAD
LONDON, S.E.18

TELEPHONE
WOOLWICH 1223
TELEGRAMS
MATCHLESS·LONDON·TELEX
TELEX No. 2-2617
CODES
ABC 5ᵗʰ & 6ᵗʰ Edⁿˢ & BENTLEYS

Our Ref ....RC/PT

Your Ref ....

22nd July, 1958.

Mr. W.A. Cakebread,
13, Bawtree Road,
New Cross,
LONDON. S.E.14.

Dear Mr. Cakebread,

Re:- <u>Apprenticeship Scheme.</u>

With reference to your interview with our Selection
Committee, I am very pleased to inform you that the
members were unanimous in their decision that you should
be admitted to our Apprenticeship Scheme.

I will be glad therefore if you will arrange to
commence work here at 9.a.m. on Monday, 1st September 1958,
bringing with you your Birth Certificate and National
Insurance Card which can be obtained from your local office
of the Ministry of National Insurance.

Will you please advise your Local Youth Employment
Office that you are commencing work here.

Yours faithfully.,
ASSOCIATED MOTOR CYCLES LTD.,

(R. Coomber)
PERSONNEL MANAGER.

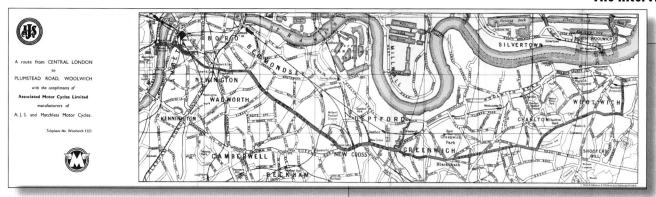

The company printed a neat fold-out map for customers that, coincidentally, showed my route to work from Central London.

hopeless nervousness and lack of academic qualifications. This interview was just too important to fail. I like to think that I won the apprenticeship on my own merit, but I can't help thinking that there were several genuine motorcycle enthusiasts sitting on that selection board and that they may have been influenced a little by my Father, quietly sitting to one side in his trench coat and waders, with gauntlets and cap clasped neatly in his lap. The company was staffed by many enthusiasts, and we were surely a family of genuine motorcyclists.

Eventually, the treasured letter arrived. The starting pay was a heady one pound nineteen shillings and six pence (£1.95) for a five day week, 8.00am to 6.00pm. Some called it slave labour. Only one thing was important, though; I had a job ... I was in ... I had a start!

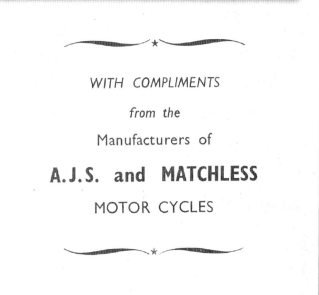

WITH COMPLIMENTS

from the

Manufacturers of

A.J.S. and MATCHLESS

MOTOR CYCLES

Opposite: The letter of appointment.

4 Before my time

It was some time after the initial excitement of securing my first employment that the t 0rue scale of the company I had joined finally dawned on my consciousness. I actually had a job with one of the largest motorcycle manufacturers in the country, and the dream was becoming a reality.

The Riley motor car company, which manufactured bicycles from 1896 and cars from 1898, proudly used the slogan 'As old as the industry.' What then of Matchless? The Collier family was manufacturing bicycles under the Matchless name in Plumstead from 1891, and motorized cycles from 1899. A similar epithet could be applied with equal justification.

The original company was founded by Henry Herbert Collier in 1878, and when his two eldest sons joined him in the business, it became H Collier and Sons. Their first attempt at motorizing one of their bicycles had the engine placed in an unsuitable position (over the front wheel), but it was soon moved to under the front down tube, and finally into the traditional diamond-shaped frame with which we're all familiar. They used De Dion and Puteaux engines and, when this company focused its interest on motor cars, Colliers continued to use the English version of the same engine marketed by MMC. Even in those early days, Colliers was advanced in its thinking and was using Longuemare spray carburettors rather than the surface type. Other early innovations included the introduction of a pillion seat in 1903, and chain drive as early as 1905. The company also introduced a tri-car in 1904, with the passenger seated between the front wheels, but this did not become a successful product line.

The founder, H H Collier, had three sons, Henry (H A – known as Harry), Charlie, and Bert (H W). All three were very competitive riders, and the father and sons must have made a formidable team during the early days of motorcycle racing. Having decided that competition was a good way to promote their products, they entered the fray with zeal, and introduced a larger machine using a V-twin by that other famous London

company, JAP at Tottenham. Their early competition events took place on the London cycle tracks at Canning Town and Crystal Palace, where motorcycle races were a natural development of the cycle races of the time. On these circuits they became

associated with another competitor, Bert (H V) Colver. The Colver family was almost as much a part of the company as the Collier brothers themselves, and continued long after the Colliers had departed the scene. Bert and his son Jack were keen competitors and remained with the company throughout their working lives. They were very much respected in the factory, and both father and son were still employed during my time there. Returning to the past, however, it was still only 1905 and already some Matchless machines had leading link front forks and swinging arm rear suspension!

1905 was also the year that marked a significant event in motorcycle competition history. In that year, eldest son Harry qualified to represent Great Britain in the International Cup motorcycle races in France. Prophetically, the eliminating trials for this race were held in the Isle of Man. The rules, however, were rather strange, the regulations stipulating a maximum weight limit of 50kg (110lb). This encouraged freak motorcycles with oversize engines in fragile frames, machines that could not be similar to the products sold to the general public. Harry and Charlie both went to France to watch the races that year; the event being won by a team from Austria.

The following year, the Austrians were the organizers of the races and both Harry and Charlie entered. The Austrians won again, but Charlie claimed a creditable third place. The Marquis

de Mouzilly de St Mars had been the British Team Manager that year, standing in for the Hon. Leopold Canning of the RAC's Auto Cycle Club. On the return journey to England, an historic meeting took place on the train.

The Collier brothers had been accompanied on this trip by their Father and, during the journey, H H Collier voiced his unhappiness about the regulations to the Marquis. They discussed alternatives, such as cubic capacity or fuel consumption as being more appropriate comparators for touring machines which the public could buy. The Marquis was obviously impressed by the discussion, and his influence must have been effective. The Auto Cycle Union agreed to organize the races, the Isle of Man agreed to close its roads for the event, and last, but not least, the generous Marquis agreed to put up a trophy for the winner, to be known as a 'Tourist Trophy.' The TT races had been born!

In 1907, the first TT races took place on the Isle of Man, and it's popularly reported that the race winner was Rem Fowler riding a Norton twin-cylinder machine powered by a Peugeot engine. This report continues to this day, and was widely repeated during the centenary celebrations in 2007. In fact, the Norton won the larger twin-cylinder class in 1907, but the overall race was won by Charlie Collier on a single-cylinder Matchless!

The Matchless was powered by a JAP overhead valve engine and averaged 38.23mph (64.72kph) and 94.5mpg (35.19km/l).

Harry Collier winning in 1909. (Courtesy Mortons)

The frontage in Plumstead Road as it was in the Colliers' time and still recognizable to the end. (Courtesy Greenwich Heritage Centre)

The class-winning Norton averaged the lower speed of 36.22mph (61.32kph) but made the fastest lap of the race at 42.91mph (72.65kph). Both machines were using the latest Brown & Barlow carburettor. The Norton used the latest Bosch magneto ignition, while the Matchless relied on an accumulator. I suspect that the lighter weight and more nimble handling of the single-cylinder machine may have been an advantage. Also, the JAP engine was more technically advanced as it employed positively operated overhead valves, while the Peugeot engine was still using the less efficient atmospheric inlet and side exhaust valve arrangement of the earlier generation of engines. The Norton was undoubtedly faster, and it did set the fastest lap, but it suffered several stoppages due to an accident caused by a burst front tyre and multiple plug changes. Perhaps our perception of that early race win is distorted by the fact that the Norton alone survives as a working museum exhibit that is still capable of being ridden. The equally famous Matchless of Charlie

Before my time

Bert Collier's personal copy of *American Machinists' Handbook* (1920 edition), the engineer's standard reference book, recovered from the AMC scrapheap.

became a Limited Company. The competition successes continued, and both Harry and Charlie had achieved TT wins by 1910. Charlie had come in second in 1908, and Harry had won at 49.0mph (82.96kph) in 1909. In 1910 Charlie came in first again at 50.63mph (85.72kph), with his brother Harry coming in second behind him. It had been a truly impressive record for the family. The newly opened Brooklands track provided yet further scope for the brothers' exploits. It was the venue where Charlie achieved the record for the 'World's Fastest Motorcycle,' recording 91.37mph (154.69kph) on a 998cc (60.85 cubic inch) V-twin for the flying mile in 1911. It was also where his less prominent younger brother, Bert, was a regular competitor during the 1920s.

The last TT successes came in the following year, 1912, when Harry and Charlie finished in third and fourth places, respectively, in the senior race. At around that time, the family moved the business from the original converted stables in Herbert Road to a more spacious wooden building at the foot of the hill leading up from the river to Plumstead Common. It was to become the established site for the factory for the next 57 years. Back at the factory, development continued unabated, and Matchless announced the first engine that was entirely of its own manufacture. It was a 3.5hp

Collier sadly appears to have passed into oblivion and thus out of the consciousness of the current generation. The Matchless achievement should not be forgotten, though, and Charlie's name was still the first to adorn that famous trophy.

Another change came in 1908 when the Colliers' business

25

Harry (H A) Collier at his desk in later years.
(Courtesy Mortons)

85.5 bore x 85.0 stroke single that, perhaps unsurprisingly, was similar to the JAP engine that it replaced. This only catered for a small part of production, however, and the company continued to use both MAG and JAP engines up to the start of the First World War. That momentous event meant that production of motorcycles ceased for the duration of the war. Perhaps surprisingly, the company won no major contracts to supply motorcycles for the armed forces, and production was switched to the manufacture of munitions and aircraft parts. Bearing in mind the company's close proximity to the Royal Arsenal, being just outside the wall, it must have felt like an extension of that vast centre of munitions manufacture. It did introduce a V-twin 'war model' in 1917, which was aimed at sidecar work and was used as a machine gun carrier, but few seem to have been made.

When civilian motorcycle manufacture began again in 1919, it was this machine, now called the 'Victory' model on which production was based, and only V-twins for sidecar use were made. It was not until 1923 that a solo machine was reintroduced, and this was the 348cc (21.21 cubic inch) model L. It seems strange that a company so steeped in solo competition before the war should take an additional five years to re-start the manufacture of solo machines. Once solo manufacture resumed, so did competition activity. Jimmy Guthrie rode a model M in the Junior TT, but the pre-war successes were elusive. The company tried once again in 1926, this time using a 347cc (21.16 cubic inch) single with an overhead camshaft engine, but once more it was without success. It's perhaps fitting that this was also the year that the father and founder of the company, H H Collier passed away. At least he must have been confident that the company was now in the hands of his three very competent sons, and the company was re-named Matchless Motorcycles (Colliers) Ltd.

In 1928, an entirely new range was designed by Harry. The machines had very advanced specifications, and included the 'Silver Arrow' for 1930. This was a unique machine which used a 397cc (24.21 cubic inch) narrow (26 degree) side valve V-twin in a fully sprung frame. In 1931, for the first time, the famous capital 'M' monogram badge was used (but without the flying wings) and a yet more sophisticated bike joined the range. This time it was the beautiful 'Silver Hawk,' a V-four with overhead camshaft drive of 593cc (36.16 cubic inch). These advanced machines showed technical prowess but, unfortunately, the conservative market was not ready for them. They were ahead of their time and, even if they had been competitive, neither machine had been designed with a capacity suitable for the classes used in competition. Production of the 'Silver Arrow' ceased in 1933, and by 1935 both machines had passed into history.

Expansion of the South London plant continued when, in 1931, the Matchless Company acquired one of its major and most respected competitors, AJS, and moved the production to Plumstead. The AJS marque had a successful competition history of its own, and it was to prove to be an interesting and

most successful association of designs. The company had ruled out racing activities and it was a strange event that brought about a change. AJS works rider, George Rowley, had joined the Collier brothers and had converted one of the 1930 overhead cam TT machines into a trials bike for the 1932 International Six Days Trial in Italy, where he was part of the British team that won the event. However, the return of the bike was delayed and the freight company imposed an additional £10 transport charge. The Colliers had little interest in the machine and refused to pay. Unbeknown to them, however, George Rowley went secretly to Dover, paid the £10, and brought the bike back to the factory where it was hidden. He then prepared it and entered it for the 100 miles Grand Prix at Brooklands.

When the Colliers discovered this they were furious, but he achieved fifth place in the junior and seventh in the senior race. On his return to the factory he was expecting to be dismissed but, instead, the brothers congratulated him. Furthermore, the directors announced that they had decided to reverse the established policy and return to racing! They would build sufficient racing machines for sale to finance the racing activities. Thus, development of the overhead camshaft AJS continued under the Plumstead management and, by 1934, the power unit, with its magneto now mounted behind the cylinder barrel, was looking very much like the post-war 7R. By 1938, with the development of the supercharged V-four (and the later Porcupine) using the AJS badge, no one could doubt that this famous marque would retain its identity under the new ownership.

The expansion continued in 1938 with the acquisition of the Sunbeam Company, and the company was again renamed, becoming that of my new employer, Associated Motor Cycles Ltd. Around the time of this change, the Matchless monogram finally grew its wings. The Second World War then intervened and the beginning was marked by two significant events. First, the Sunbeam Company was sold to the BSA Group in 1943, and, sadly, the youngest brother, Bert, was killed in a road accident. This war was different from the last in that production of motorcycles for the military was maintained throughout. Over 80,000 350cc (21.34 cubic inch) G3L models were produced for the armed forces. Technical development also continued, and from 1941 these were fitted with the patented 'Teledraulic' telescopic forks in place of the traditional girder type. In 1944 the war in Europe ended, and the eldest Collier brother, Harry, died, leaving Charlie as the sole survivor of the founding family.

The share capital of the company was doubled in 1947 and the expansion of Associated Motor Cycles Ltd continued after the war with the acquisition of Norton, Francis Barnet, and James. Racing took centre stage again when the war ended with a bold attempt to introduce the supercharged 'Porcupine' works racer, thwarted almost immediately by the ban on the use of superchargers. However, 1948 saw the introduction of the famous 'Boy Racer' 350cc (21.34 cubic inch) AJS, a beautifully engineered motorcycle from the pen of Phil Walker, AMC employee and designer of the pre-war overhead camshaft AJS. If there had ever been any doubt in AJS enthusiasts' minds about what Matchless might do with the competitor's name it had acquired, then they must surely have been dispelled with

The AJS 7R 'Boy Racer.'

The Matchless G45 twin.

the introduction of the immortal 7R. The racing bikes were catalogued items available for anyone to buy.

A 500cc (30.49 cubic inch) vertical twin followed in 1949 which incorporated the unique feature of having separate cylinder barrels and heads. A racing version, known as the Matchless G45, appeared in 1951, and once again Matchless returned to the Isle of Man. It was not for the TT races this time, however, but for the Amateur Manx Grand Prix. Robin Sherry acquitted himself well on the G45 by finishing fourth in the senior race, and the following year Derek Farrant won the race outright on another G45. Meanwhile, in the junior 350cc (21.34 cubic inch) class, Bob McIntyre won the 1952 Manx Grand Prix, and came second in the senior race on the same machine! A three-valve version of the 7R AJS, the 7R3, was designed by consultant Ike Hatch and developed by Jack Williams in 1952. This rare and complex engine did not perhaps receive the development that it deserved, but with Rod Coleman riding, it won the Junior TT in 1954, bringing to an end a five-year run of Norton successes. It was a good note to end on, and Charlie, the last remaining of the Collier brothers, died at his desk at the factory that same year.

Charlie Collier was always known in the factory as 'Mr Charlie' and, when I joined four years later, he was still spoken about with much reverence. However, his friend and associate, Bert Colver, who had been with him from the start, was still very much a part of the daily activity. He provided a continuous link to the history of the company that I was now proud to be a part of.

5 Drilling Shop initiation

The appointed start date of Monday 1st September 1958 duly arrived and school holidays had gone forever. Some of the time I rode my motorcycle to work, but finances dictated that on other days I cycled. I was still unable to afford proper motorcycling clothing, but on this special occasion I rode to work on the BSA. Every journey was an enjoyment and the daily ride to work no less so. Each day presented a new challenge, glorious sunshine or icy roads. Every journey was different, a small adventure in itself.

The welcome was formal in the Personnel Manager's office. I was introduced to the routines of tea and lunch breaks, and told of the arrangements made for me to attend day-release at the South East London Technical College. There, I was to study for an Ordinary National Certificate in Mechanical Engineering and, if I was good enough, would go on to study for the Higher National Certificate. Some hopes, I thought quietly to myself, the memories of recent academic failures still fresh in my mind. My only consolation to being sent back to school was that it would be like a day off, a shorter day. The college was much closer to my home than the factory was so I could lie in bed a little longer (I never did like getting up).

The formalities over, and clutching my ridiculously clean bib-and-brace overalls to my side, I was taken through the factory to be introduced to the Drilling Shop Manager. He seemed a kindly enough person but rather disinterested in this new charge that had been foisted on him. The addition of a new apprentice to his workforce was clearly not regarded as a benefit. I later discovered that, in the factory, the Drilling Shop was considered the lowest of the low. The department that was able to employ the least skilled labour force. Among the regular and kindly family men like my father was a smattering of dropouts and ex-convicts. To me at that time, though, they were all highly skilled people from whom I could learn much. To be a machine operator like them would be an achievement, one step higher than my poor father

who, for reasons of his own choosing rather than lack of ability, had remained a storekeeper in the same Merryweathers stores for the whole of his working life. I had the utmost respect for him, but he was totally devoid of ambition and, in this way, he was very different from the two sons that he sired.

When, at morning tea-break one day, I was asked by a group of workers what I wanted to be, my innocent and sincere reply was, "A machine operator like you." My response was met with laughter and derision. They explained that an apprenticeship should lead me to much greater possibilities than that. It was something that I had not contemplated before. Was it really possible for me to achieve more? I thought not.

The apprentice scheme was such that you were scheduled to spend three to six months in each department before graduating to the higher echelons of the tool room, and then finally spending some of the last year in the discipline of your choice. If you were good enough at the end of the five years, there might be the possibility of permanent employment.

The first month or so of my training was spent in pure boredom. Lack of interest on the part of the shop management meant that I was set to watch the various operators use the drills, taps, automatic reversing heads and various jigs and fixtures. I suppose that I was learning something by watching, but I really wanted to get on the tools myself and have a go. Because the machine shops all worked on a piecework system, however, time was critical for the operators to earn their money, and there was no opportunity for them to stop and let me have a try. The work that the apprentices were allowed to do was by definition rather menial.

Without realizing it, I had, in fact, learned a great deal about the essential use of jigs and fixtures in a production environment. The use of interchangeable 'slip' bushes to drill, tap or counter-bore a hole in the same position, and the supreme art of changing tools 'on the fly' without stopping the spindle (and without dropping the tools!) using quick-change chucks were all skills that I learned, eventually mastered, and took some pleasure from that achievement.

To explain the piece-work system and the need for this speed, each operation was timed with a stopwatch by a 'time and motion' man to set a 'standard time' for the job. A bonus rate was paid in proportion to the production rate that was achieved above this standard. Naturally, an operator went as slowly as possible when being timed, taking deliberate care to use all of the safety guards provided and religiously cleaning the swarf away before picking up the next part to be machined. When it came to production, however, the guards were dispensed with, and every effort was made to machine as many parts as possible in the minimum time. It was usually possible to earn 'double time' bonus (i.e. doing the job in half the allotted time),

often to earn 'treble time,' and occasionally, by working very hard, to achieve 'square time' (four times as fast as the official time). A regular incidence of 'square time' jobs, however, raised suspicion about the authenticity of the timings, and it was wise to avoid achieving this level of bonus too often!

The good thing about the drilling shop is that it was on the ground floor of the four storey factory, near the lift. The various machine shops with their heavy machinery were spread throughout the four floors, and the bikes themselves were assembled on the second floor. The large goods lift had a permanent operator and served all floors, including the roof. A smaller and additional 'roof shop,' like a brick shed on the roof of the building, was used for making cables, brazing, welding and fettling castings, etc.

The lift had folding doors at each end, one end opening

The 'Porcupine' AJS.

Motorcycle Apprentice

into the factory and one out into a small yard and the gated entrance in Maxey Road. It would typically hold about six bikes and there would be a constant stream of machines going down for testing/delivery or back up for rectification of faults. It was the sight of all those lovely new bikes and the thought of my closer involvement with them in the future that kept me motivated.

It was not many weeks before the realization of my dream began, but it was to turn into a bitter memory of an act of vandalism that would haunt me for the rest of my life. I was overjoyed when another apprentice and I were selected to escape from the drilling shop boredom to work for a short while in the 'holy of holies,' the Race Shop.

Not many of the regular workers ever saw the inside of the Race Shop, as its work was shrouded in secrecy. Along with the Packing Shop, Spares Department, and employees' car park, it was separated from the main four-storey factory by Burrage Grove that ran parallel to Plumstead Road, where the main offices were fronted by a simple and rather nondescript shop front.

The race shop was a single storey rectangular building with its narrow side facing the road. At the front end, bordering the road, it was occupied by the Competition Department where 'works' trials and scrambles bikes were assembled under the expert direction of Wally Wyatt. The main body of the shop was given over to the assembly of 7Rs and G50s, with an office at the back occupied by the kindly, boffin-like Jack Williams. Above his office was a short mezzanine floor that was the Race Shop spares store. Out at the back and underground were two caverns, accessed by vertical steel ladders, which housed the Heenan and Froude water-brake dynamometers where the race and development engines were individually tested.

On this occasion, however, we were only allowed access to the store above the office, with only sneaky looks at the race bike preparation going on below. Our task was a simple one, to clear some space in the stores by getting rid of the stock of obsolete spares. They were to be taken down and transported to the main factory in a wheelbarrow and then destroyed before being placed on the scrap heap that occupied the corner of the yard to the right of the lift.

We were shown how to operate a fly press to best destructive effect. It was a vandal's delight! Even I was surprised, however, when the parts to be destroyed looked so intricate and perfect and even more surprised when we found that the stock included complete and beautifully stove enamelled frames. We were given special instruction on these, how to break their backs on a larger press to make sure that they could not be re-used. At the time, we did not recognize the parts as belonging to any motorcycle that we knew, and did as we were instructed.

The scrap heap was a useful source of materials and, therefore, a popular place for the workers to congregate near the new bikes at lunchtime and tea-breaks. It was only the reaction of the workers when they arrived that made us realize that we were destroying something that was dear to them. Some workers scrounged souvenirs of intricate machined parts from us, while others, more closely connected with the racing scene, appeared to be significantly distressed.

Slowly we learned that we were destroying the last remnants of the fabulous 'Porcupine' AJS, the factory's last effort at serious works Grand Prix racing. I later discovered that there was one complete but uncared for example still at the factory (it was sometimes left outside in the rain propped up against a wall!) and a sectioned engine was on a stand in the Drawing Office. Apart from these, we had just destroyed all else that remained, probably enough parts to build several bikes. I felt guilty and tainted and went back to the mundane business of the Drilling Shop where worse experiences were waiting.

At first it seemed like some good news was awaiting me. I was to work directly with a chargehand who would take me under his wing and teach me. I will spare his name. He was a heavily built and militant union man. He gave me a hard time for refusing to join the union, and an even harder time on the machines. He 'taught' me nothing, but constantly left me to my own devices. Some cast-iron cylinder barrels, for instance, had tapped holes for the head studs. The tapping holes would have been jig-drilled previously, but the tapping was done free-hand using an automatic reversing head on the drill to bring the tap back out of the hole. A delicate touch was needed to judge when you had tapped deep enough (too deep and the tap would 'bottom' in the hole and break). Bring the pressure off too soon by not balancing the return spring pressure on the handle of the drilling machine, and the cylinder would lift off the bed and snap the tap like a carrot. His method of 'teaching' was to give no demonstration, but to watch as I broke tap after tap and then roll about laughing at my lack of skill. He made me feel that I was incapable of doing anything. It was the lowest point in my apprenticeship, and it had come so soon. I was so anxious to be a success, so keen not to fail, so tired by the journey to work and the long working days, and so depressed by the destruction of the Porcupines, I hit rock bottom. Ashamed as I am to admit it, I cried. I hate to think what that man cost the company in broken tools but, however much it was, it seemed to be of little concern to him. The experience made me think that I would never be able to cope with factory life, but somehow I gritted my teeth and returned day after miserable tiring day to face the tyrant and to do his bidding.

His comeuppance was not far away. One of my duties as his apprentice, of course, was to do all of his work for him. His day was mostly spent idly chatting or smoking outside by the lift doors. He also liked a drink or two. Just across the road from the side gate near the lift was a pub on the corner of Plumstead and Maxey Roads. While I was doing his work for him, he would quietly disappear. Everyone knew where he would be. One of his sole responsibilities was the big boring machine that was used to machine the cylinder barrels. It was the largest machine in the shop, with two massive vertical cutting spindles. I admit that in this instance he did take great care to teach me how to operate this one, presumably to ensure that his leisure time remained secure. The machine had a huge circular bed with three positions, one for the 'rough cut' spindle, one for the second 'fine cut' spindle, and the third, nearest to the operator, was the change-over position. Two cylinder barrels were thus bored simultaneously (one rough and one fine cut) while the operator removed one finished bored cylinder and replaced it with a new raw casting. An enormous signal-box like lever mechanism unlatched the table to allow it to rotate between operations, and one very important aspect of operating this monster was to use a little tin shovel located under each fixture to remove the swarf that had been produced before fitting a new casting. After my depressing experience in the Drilling Shop, I guess that I became a little proud and perhaps a little over confident when this puny youth mastered the most complex machine in the department and was left alone with it day after day.

On the day of the disaster we were machining cylinder liners for the 7R and G50 racers. In my newly found confidence, I was blissfully unaware amongst all the din in the machine shop that one sound was making itself heard above all of the others, so much so, in fact, it could apparently be heard in the pub across the road! Seemingly from nowhere, my mentor suddenly appeared by my side, red faced and puffing. He slammed his fist on the emergency stop button; and suddenly it was quieter.

Now, 7R and G50 cylinders weren't made from a normal finned casting. They were machined from a very thick-walled liner that was later shrunk into the finned aluminium shroud of the cylinder barrel. The cut was, therefore, much heavier than normal, and the generation of swarf was correspondingly higher. All it had taken was one bored, over confident moment, for me to forget to clear the swarf away when I fitted a fresh casting. When the all-powerful boring head came inexorably down, there was nowhere for the new swarf to go, and so the boring head compressed it in the cylinder until the machine's bearings screamed for relief! The resulting disaster couldn't be disguised. The machine would not back-up. The liners had split

and expanded in the fixture. The whole machine was locked solid. It took days to get it working again.

I suffered no criticism. After all, I'd only been working for the company for a few weeks. I was just 17 years of age and fresh out of school. What was I doing there, operating such a machine without supervision anyway? To my eternal surprise, I received no punishment for my error, and didn't even receive any recrimination from the chargehand. In fact, he treated me carefully, and with more respect after that incident, and actually took care to try to teach me something. I don't know exactly what happened with him over the matter, but I am pleased that he kept his job and I managed to survive to the end of my term in that Drilling Shop. Many years later, after the factory had closed, Bernard Copleston, another apprentice, related a story to me about the same man and how grateful he had been for the skills that he had learned from him. He was talking specifically about the ability that we shared in being able to sharpen drills of all sizes by eye without assistance from any special grinding machines or tools. I had acquired this particular skill in the Tool Room, but Bernard had been taught by this particular chargehand. There was a sting in the tail of the story, however, for when, after many failed attempts, the chargehand finally agreed that the drill in question had been sharpened to perfection, he had immediately thrust it into the grinding wheel and destroyed it. "There, now that you have proved you can do it, you can do it all again." I suppose that it's one method of teaching, but I certainly didn't appreciate it at the time. That department was in the very bottom corner of the building, next to the scrap heap. The only way was up!

Visit Veloce on the web – www.veloce.co.uk
Details of all books in print • Special offers • New book news • Gift vouchers

33

6 Heat Treatment – a man's world

If I'd been shaken by my initiation into factory work in the Drilling Shop, the prospect of my next transfer scared me to death. My confidence had taken a battering. I felt weakened and ill-prepared for the challenge that confronted me. My next move was to be to the Heat Treatment Department next door, located on the ground floor adjacent to the Drilling Shop, on the other side of the lift. Passing by, it had seemed like Hades itself, with fiery furnaces, dust and heat. Manned by rough looking men working partially stripped, even in winter, it seemed no place for a novice apprentice like me, still wet behind the ears. Based on my recent experiences in the Drilling Shop, I expected the worst.

A row of rectangular, iron clad, gas fired ovens lined the left-hand wall. Each oven had a heavy cast iron door freely suspended on chains in case of explosion with a chain hoist on each to raise and lower them. On the far right was the gas carburizing plant, a large cylinder, perhaps 15 feet (5 metres) in diameter, set mainly below ground fitted with a huge lid. Its workings were a mystery. The centre of the floor was occupied by a row of much smaller cyanide hardening plants, open water and oil tanks for quenching and a working area where parts to be case hardened were packed and sealed in containers for conventional carburizing in the ovens. At the entrance stood the Foreman's office and a large board full of pyrometer dials monitoring the temperature in each of the ovens.

This time, my introduction was more civilized, the Foreman, Jack Godley, taking care to explain exactly what I was there to learn. He took a genuine interest in everything that I did, and occasionally tested me with questions about the different processes. On his advice, I started to keep a notebook, learned how to tell the temperature of the oven by its colour, and a host of other useful information about hardening and tempering of various metals. I was learning something new and suddenly this began to feel like an apprenticeship.

Much to my surprise, I didn't find the heat and dirt a hardship.

To the contrary, I revelled in the challenge to be able to act like a real man and, under the workers' guidance, I did everything that they did. For the first time, praise came from the Foreman and I stood tall once again. The men in the Heat Treatment Shop explained to me that my former chargehand's character and communist leanings were well known. Now, with the realization that the experience was not due to my personal failure, and that I was not alone, I was able to put the Drilling Shop incidents into proper perspective and behind me.

Jokes on apprentices are all a part of factory life and, from the start, I was wary of not being made a fool of by being sent to the Stores for a '⅝ hole' or 'a long weight' (wait), etc. Once, however, in the Heat Treatment Department, my caution backfired on me.

It must be recognized that the most vulnerable part, and the crowning glory, of a motorcycle is the petrol tank. It does not take much imagination, therefore, to work out that they were frequently scratched and needed repair. In later years, the testers used special test tanks, holding only a pint or two of fuel that were made from the cylindrical tool boxes used on the trials bikes. They were clamped horizontally across the top tube of the frame with an oil cap serving as a filler cap. The bikes looked very sporty when ridden without a fuel tank and the whole engine exposed!

One thing that AMC was rightly proud of was the quality of its stove enamelling and, when necessary, the method of removing the paint was to burn it off. This is where the apprentice came into the story. The conventional way to heat treat components (hardening or tempering) was to lay them on a heavy steel tray and, with a pair of very long steel tongs, pick up the tray and place it in the pre-heated oven. The operation was very much like that of a baker's oven. When all of the components had reached the required temperature, the red-hot components would be withdrawn and tipped into one of the quenching tanks

Jack Godley, Foreman of the Heat Treatment Department, attends the nitriding furnace.

for hardening, or left on the floor to cool if they were required to be tempered or annealed.

The fuel tanks were quite light and it was possible to fit several to a tray. With the oven set with its brick lining glowing a dull red, I was instructed how long to leave them in to remove the paint and was left with the oven and a pile of damaged tanks. I picked up the first tank and, to my horror, heard petrol swilling about in the bottom! Now this, I thought, was an apprentice joke taken too far. To be laughed at is one thing, to be blown to pieces, quite another. I refused to do it, of course, and finally the Foreman was sent for. He calmly reassured me, placed the tanks on the tray, opened the hot oven door, and placed them in the oven himself. There was no explosion, only a low 'woomf'

sound as a sheet of flame licked out from under the open oven door. It seems that the sudden heat of the oven caused the fuel to expand and vapourize very quickly so that it was only ignited by the flames as it exited the filler neck, rather than inside the tank itself, as one would expect. I had learned something new but to this day have often wondered if the first person to place a tank with fuel in it into the oven did it by accident, rather than intention!

My time in this harsh department gave me a boost in confidence and a genuine desire to learn for the first time in many years. Suddenly, I found work interesting and a career in heat treatment and metallurgy seemed a possibility: for now, though, I had to go back to school.

7 An accident, setback & recovery

Now a fully fledged factory worker, owning his own motorbike, spring was coming and the world was at my feet. Everything was possible. The only previous race meetings that I can recall ever having attended were those, accessible by bicycle, held at Crystal Palace, and the occasional trip with my Father to see a scramble or hillclimb at Knats Valley near Brands Hatch.

The first real race meeting of the year to be held at Brands Hatch was, therefore, an eagerly awaited 'must' on the calendar. When the day finally dawned, however, it was bitterly cold, with ice and snow on the ground. Mum and Dad had already planned to visit my uncle Alf (Dad's eldest brother) and his family at Eltham, which was en route to Brands Hatch, and it was arranged that we would meet up there for some tea and a ride home together in convoy when I'd finished my day at the races.

All of the local 'hard men,' with their Dominators, Gold Stars and Tiger 110s, were planning to go, all complete with their clip-on handlebars, big boots, leather jackets and white sub-mariners socks and scarves. My paltry outfit consisted of a PVC jacket with leaky seams, thin waterproof overtrousers, rubber Wellington boots, and a pair of gloves rather than gauntlets. Wearing this outfit and riding the side-valve BSA, I would hardly be cutting a dash with the neighbourhood bikers, but just being there was the important thing. I was keen to be seen as one of the real motorcyclists.

I met up with the local crowd from New Cross on the outside of Clearways bend, just before the finish straight. I tried hard to be interested in the racing, but in truth, for most of the time, I was too numb with the cold. Instead of enjoying the big adventure, I was relieved when the light began to fade and it was time to leave. More snow had fallen, though, and the road out of the circuit was treacherous. I had almost gained the main road when I 'lost it' on the ice. Both the bike and I were deposited unceremoniously in a ditch filled with snow.

No-one seemed to notice me as, muffled against the wind,

they struggled for their own survival in the blizzard-like conditions. Eventually, tired and totally exhausted, I managed to drag that heavy bike back onto the road, dried the ignition and re-started it. Only then did I discover that both my gloves and scarf were missing, buried in the snow by my efforts to retrieve the bike. Now too tired to care, I decided that home and warmth were the only important targets in my life, and I set out for the security and warmth of my uncle's home.

The icy wind now entered the many openings in my inadequate clothes. It whistled up my arms and down my neck. My fingers went numb and I shivered involuntarily. My mind focused only on the destination ahead as I prayed that I wouldn't fall off a second time. When I finally reached the rest of my family, sitting in the warmth of my uncle's lounge, I somehow could not get warm again. After a suitable dose of hot tea and something to eat, there was a debate as to whether I should abandon my bike and travel home in the relative comfort of the sidecar. Stupid pride and the determination to see it through, however, made me insist on completing the journey back to New Cross. It was a decision that I was to regret for a very long time, perhaps even for the rest of my life.

There was no work for me the next morning, nor was there to be for many weeks to come. The doctor had been called to attend to my uncontrolled shivering and fever and pronounced the cause to be bronchial pneumonia. I stayed in bed and hated motorcycles. When I finally ventured out of my bedroom several weeks later, I couldn't bear the thought of facing that machine again. I was moved, however, when I looked out of the back window to see my Father carefully cleaning the mud and salt from my bike. He had no love for solos and had never previously touched it. I felt grateful but remote and more than a little guilty that, despite his efforts, I had so little interest in riding it again.

Brought up in smog-laden London, breathing ailments were common, but from that day on, I suffered continuous bouts of bronchitis until the damage was finally diagnosed as emphysema by our family doctor. This was a terrible blow, and there followed many visits to chest clinics and hospitals in London over the following years. The illness did have its lighter moments. No-one in the family had heard of emphysema previously, but my Mother and Father were proud of their collection of books. They were mostly about the British Empire and the Second World War with the obligatory set of *Encyclopaedia Britannica*, purchased for our education, but never read, of course. They were housed in a highly polished and locked bookcase that had (characteristically) been made by my Father out of the case of an old piano.

Amongst these books was a medical dictionary to which my dear Mother instantly referred. Unfortunately, she unwisely did so without caution, and read aloud to the assembled family the most depressing prognosis for my life that could be imagined. The family looked on in grim silence as she read this prophesy of doom and progressively deteriorating health. Not knowing what to say at the end of it, she looked up and said, "There now, that's not so bad, is it?" We all looked at each other in disbelief and burst out laughing. The ice was broken. There was only one thing left to do now and that was to fight it and try to get better.

The apprenticeship had been disrupted by the illness and, to my eternal regret, I missed out on the training for welding. Once on my feet again, my reaction was to turn against my long love affair with motorcycles and turn my attention to the relative comfort of a car. This idea was met with utter amazement in the family. No member of the family had ever owned a car before. I have previously referred to my father's lack of personal ambition. In many ways, he was the most contented man that I ever knew. He was basically a happy man and always seemed to be satisfied with what he had. We had been brought up with the understanding that cars were for rich people, and that we belonged to a different class that wasn't meant to own motor cars. To have ideas above one's station in life was not helpful.

For me, though, ambition knew no limits, and I knew that it should not be just any car, but a sports car, no less! The family's amazement was replaced by disbelief. The BSA was sold and the money was put towards my first MG, purchased from Levy's, one of the numerous dealers operating from the many bomb sites in and around Lewisham at the time. It was a rather down-at-heel M-type of 1930 vintage, fitted with a Ford side-valve engine and with the rather wonderful registration mark

Motorcycling companions Ray McElhinney and school friend Dave Jackman on the Eltham by-pass.

The 'M' type MG pointing toward the exit road from the garages. In the background, my father surveys the scene from the balcony at the back of our flat.

of JO 95. Painted red, and with its pointed tail, it looked very racy to my eyes. I had no idea how I would learn to drive it, or afford to run it, but I had my first car! I tried to put to the back of my mind that from now on I had to cycle to work everyday; oh the price of vanity!

I must have been a car dealer's dream customer. With no knowledge whatsoever of motorcars, no friends with any experience, and no-one in the family to advise, my lessons were to be learned the hard way. The same dealer had a flat-radiator Morgan a few weeks before, but that had been out of reach financially. There was also a little Austin Nippy at the back of a car lot opposite the end of Brookmill Road in Lewisham that I'd looked at longingly, but again, finances would not stretch that far (I think that it was £95) and I settled for what I could afford, the pretty, but totally impractical, M type MG.

Ray McElhinney was a chimney sweep's son, good friend and fellow motorcyclist whose father had just given up renting one of the Nissen hut garages at the back of our house in favour of leaving his black (of course) Ford van on the street. Ray owned a B32 BSA and we rented his father's former garage between us to store his bike and the MG. We had fun driving the MG in

the dirt yard that the garages surrounded and taught ourselves the art of clutch and gear control. We even had one daring and very illegal circuit 'round the block' on the public roads, the madness of which now horrifies me.

The reality of just how impractical the MG was slowly dawned on me, but not before that lovely pointed tail collapsed due to terminal wood-rot, and Dad once again had to come to the rescue. With the aid of more off-cuts of ash and aluminium from Merryweathers, Dad applied the coach-building skills that he had acquired by building his sidecars to the reconstruction of a new back end. Partly to make construction easier, and partly to emulate the more modern type of MG, I opted for a flat rear end this time, with an externally mounted spare wheel. Although very non-original, the result was very presentable and another credit to my Father's skills. I regret to say, however, that this particular MG never made it again onto the public roads during my ownership. It finally went back whence it came in part-exchange for LMM 271, a smart, sensible and totally boring Series 'E' Morris that was to be my second unsuccessful attempt at car ownership.

Everything looks better in the summer, and so it was that I soon became tired (physically and mentally!) of cycling or using public transport to get to work and college. Just how unrealistic my attempts at car ownership had been were now clear to me. It had been financially impractical from the beginning and I now had to submit to that fact of life. I felt stronger again and the love of motorcycling returned.

The car was sold, the borrowings repaid and the Saturday trips to the motorcycle dealers began once again. After a very stern lecture from my Mother to my Father that I was "not to be allowed to buy anything bigger than 250cc," we again found the most likely prospects in the back of Comerfords at Thames Ditton. Unfortunately for my Father, the bike that was outstanding relative to the others for condition and value was a 500cc ohv BSA B33, rigid framed and red tanked of 1949 vintage. HOY 122 was very original and, as yet, unspoiled. There was no contest. Dad weakened and received a terrible tongue lashing from my Mother on our return home. I, on the other hand, escaped relatively lightly from my Mother's scorn, and this BSA served me well for several years until I was able to move up the quality motorcycle ladder. My driving test was taken on this machine and at last I was motorcycling again! Now older and

The proud owner of a proper overhead-valve BSA B33.

Motorcycle Apprentice

wiser, I purchased a proper 'Belstaff Black Prince' motorcycle suit, waterproof overboots and decent gauntlets. Bad weather was no longer a problem, and the world with its endless roads beckoned once again.

Born into this island race, many of us have a love and a fascination, as I have, for the sea and ships. I see a similar parallel between the sea, the road and the endless possibilities of where they might lead. Sailing a small boat, there is a wonderful sense of freedom that is very tangible. Detached from the land, you're in command of your own private island and temporarily isolated from the rest of the world. The awesome fact is that even in the shallowest of our tidal waterways or creeks, we are immediately connected to salt water that is a direct route to absolutely anywhere in the world, with nothing in the way. All that you have to do is turn left or right when you reach the sea and just keep going! How many weekend sailors who probably may never venture more than a mile from the harbour entrance enjoy this sub-conscious escapist dream, I wonder?

'The Road.' What then, is the fascination of that endless strip of tarmac? T E Lawrence (of Arabia) wrote an excellent chapter by this title in his lesser known book *The Mint*, describing a journey on his Brough Superior. I could not attempt to describe it better. The road, although much more limited in its scope and ridiculously over regulated by comparison with the sea, offers a similar invitation to that freedom, whether it be real or imaginary. To see that ribbon of tarmac racing under the front wheel as the world unfolds, mile after mile, is surely the intoxicating experience that makes one keep coming back for more. There is, of course, a similar and less pleasant parallel between motorcycles and small boats at sea. The motorcyclist, on a winter night, cold and wet with gloves soaked through and fingers that he can no longer feel, would readily identify with the wave-swept lone sailor peering into the darkness on a stormy night at sea. Both, I suspect, sometimes think to themselves 'Why the **** am I doing this?'

8 College work & metallurgy

I didn't relish the thought of going back to school. The South East London Technical College was on the main road between my home at New Cross and Lewisham. A large rectangular building, it wasn't a welcoming façade, and I attended with reluctance. It was just another day away from real work and my beloved motorcycles, but it was a condition of my contracted indentures, and there was no choice. Had there been a choice, I would surely have preferred to be at work.

Strangely, however, unlike at school, the lecturer's words seemed to make sense for a change, and somehow I didn't find the understanding as difficult as I had expected. It was a vague thought that lodged in the back of my mind, but I made no effort to analyse it at the time. The revelation finally dawned on me at the end of the first academic year when the examination results were published. I had passed! It all came as a bit of a shock after all of those years of failure at the grammar school. Suddenly, for the first time since my primary school days, I was deemed to be academically capable again. Anything was now possible.

In the final analysis some time afterwards, I realised that learning had become easy again because it finally had meaning and an application. At Wilson's grammar school, the teaching had been very academic and didn't seem to relate to anything useful in the real world. A strong interest and some ability in art (I once had a picture hung in the Camberwell Art Gallery) was crushed when, halfway through the secondary education, we were forced to choose between 'art' and 'science.' As my other interest was technical, I chose science, but always regretted being forced to make this choice. I had to abandon any pursuit of languages or art, subjects that I enjoyed and, in the case of languages, skills that I would miss later in my career. To add further insult to injury, the school had no metalworking facilities, and the only practical training available was in woodwork. It's no wonder that I hated my schooling so much.

Now I enjoyed a new lease of life. Mathematics, a subject

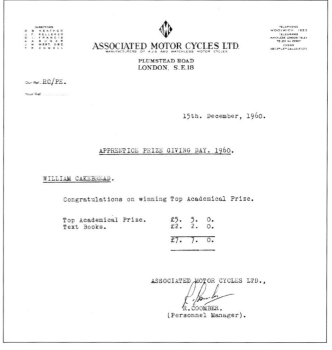

Top academic prize 1960. To my surprise, this was repeated again in 1962 with top practical award in 1961!

that made no sense to me at all at school, was suddenly easy because it had an engineering application. I wanted to understand because it was needed if I wanted to be an engineer. While in the first year of college, another transfer came due. Having earned my stripes in the Heat Treatment Department, I was moved to the softest department in the factory. Sandwiched

Motorcycle Apprentice

between the Heat Treatment Shop and the buildings that fronted onto Plumstead Road was a single storey building that was the Metallurgy Department. It was manned by the very senior and much respected Mr Eaton and a technician. Mr Eaton was a professional man, always wearing a suit and tie and mixing with top management. The dark skinned technician always wore a very clean white coat. He was both intelligent and kind and taught me all he knew in the generous amount of time that was available to us. We were not required to work too hard.

The prime functions of the department were to monitor the quality of each batch of heat-treated components, and to maintain the concentration of the cyanide baths (some small components were case hardened by a period of immersion in a hot cyanide solution). The only direct production operation performed there was the induction hardening of the ends of the

clutch pushrods. If one is unfamiliar with induction hardening, it is an intriguing process. Protruding from the steel electrical cabinet is a spiral formed out of three or four coils of copper tube that have a continuous flow of cooling water passing through them. An electrical current is passed through the coils when the machine is operated. Placing anything metallic within the coil causes it to be heated. A bunch of perhaps 6 silver-steel clutch pushrods would be held together in the hand with their ends flush with each other. The ends would be held within the coil (taking care not to let them touch the copper) until they glowed to the required colour. The ends would then be plunged into a drum of quenching oil to complete this most simple of all hardening processes. The operation would then be repeated for the other end of the rods. It was a simple and boring operation. Although definitely not recommended, it was supposed to be possible to

The rear of the factory as seen from Maxey Road. Beyond the factory roof, towards the river, can be seen the massive buildings inside the walls of the Woolwich Arsenal. (Courtesy Greenwich Heritage Centre)

place a finger in the coil without coming to harm. I never put it to the test for fear that the machine might find a metallic splinter hidden under the skin!

Measuring the case hardening depth was more interesting. A water-cooled cutting wheel would be used to carefully cut a segment out of, say, a gear wheel, and then cut a section through a few of the teeth. This sample was then moulded into a circular plastic mount to hold it before being ground and polished to a fine finish. It was then acid-etched to reveal the case hardening. The depth of the hardening would be measured with a calibrated microscope. When the sample had proved that the depth of case hardening was adequate, that batch of components would then pass on for the next operation.

There was much soul destroying idleness in that department, however. Much of the day was spent with the technician reading magazines while waiting for the next sample to be processed. The department was located in a backwater out-building between the main factory and the front office building. It was a dead-end that led to nowhere, and no one seemed to bother that we were so little occupied. Although I was inspired to emulate Mr Eaton for a while, and wanted to acquire his knowledge, I was glad when the tedium came to an end. In spite of the boredom, my interest in the subject was sustained by the experience, and later on I added Metallurgy to the list of 'endorsement subjects' to be taken with the Higher National Certificate.

One occasional event enlivened the day-to-day routine of the apprentice's life, and that was the opportunity to make outside visits to other companies to broaden our education. Two such visits were to leave lasting impressions. The first was to Ford's gigantic plant at Dagenham. We had a particular interest there as the excellently equipped AMC Gear Cutting Shop also produced gearbox internals for Ford. Apart from the sheer scale of the operation, this visit was memorable for two reasons. The first was the archaic treatment of the line workers and their/our mutual embarrassment when visiting the toilets to find the stalls were only fitted with half height stable doors so the foremen could make periodic checks for malingerers. The second was to witness the crudeness by which the doors were aligned on the new 'sloping back window' Anglia that was currently in production. My recollection is that the door hinges were welded rather than bolted to the door post in the traditional manner. Whatever the method of attachment, however, the interesting part was that the door fit in the aperture was achieved by placing a mallet head between the appropriate door hinge and post and leaning on the outer edge of the door to raise or lower it until the required fit was achieved! The method was effective but alien to my engineering sensitivity. The memory of this education was vividly brought back to me some ten years later when I was managing a draughtsman who used one such vehicle as his daily transport. I was watching from an office window when he left the car in a hurry when late arriving for work one morning. He slammed the driver's door behind him and strode purposefully towards the factory. Seconds later, the door fell off and clattered to the ground!

The other visit, memorable for a totally different reason, was to the nearby Woolwich Arsenal, much of which could be seen from the roof of our factory. This visit occurred when my interest in metallurgy was at its peak. The original AJS/Matchless 500cc (30.48 cubic inch) vertical twins had used Meehanite cast iron castings for the crankshaft. As the engines were enlarged to 600 (36.59) and subsequently 650cc (39.63 cubic inch) and developed more power, the crankshaft material was changed to 'SNG 37/2' cast iron. Interpreted, this abbreviation means 'Spheroidal Nodular Graphited' cast iron, with a tensile strength of 37 tons/square inch (5752 kilogrammes/square centimetre) and 2 per cent elongation - a much stronger and less brittle material. To me, this was a very modern cast iron, and I was, therefore, intrigued when our guide referred to the same material being used for casting the casing of grenades. I was interested why this material was chosen and was told that because of its more uniform structure, it shattered into a larger number of pieces and, therefore, would kill a greater number of people! I was saddened by the answer. How different is the world of a weapons engineer from that of a motorcycle designer! The motorcycle world suffers more than its fair share of deaths and disabilities, but at least they occur by accident rather than intent.

Twice a day, my ride to and from work took me past the entrance road that led to Stones of Charlton, the sub-contract foundry which supplied most, if not all, of the aluminium castings for the company. This was another impressive place to visit, not only for the interesting foundry techniques involved in the manufacture of our components, but to see at first hand the casting of massive bronze propellers for ocean going ships. To see the hub of one of these being machined was an even greater spectacle, the operator of a huge lathe standing on the cross-slide adjacent to the tool while the propeller blades scythed the air by his left arm like the blades of a huge wind turbine.

Visit Veloce on the web – www.veloce.co.uk
Details of all books in print • Special offers • New book news • Gift vouchers

43

9 Fun & games

The atmosphere inside the factory was mostly dark and dingy, and the floor-to-ceiling wire cages that separated some of the departments for security reasons sometimes conspired to make it feel like a prison. This was not reflected in the attitude of the workers, however, and a cheerful family ambiance is the enduring memory of most ex-employees. I once remarked to an older worker that the atmosphere was so good that I enjoyed being at work as much as being at home. His jaundiced reply was short and sweet: "You must have a bloody awful home life then!" It was not true, of course, and I was not alone in the feeling of camaraderie that existed.

Jokers abounded in every department, but especially in the Assembly and Rectification areas, it seemed. A memorable feature of this shop was the tricks played with the treacle-like grease that was used as initial lubrication for the timing chains on the single cylinder machines. It has an unusually tacky consistency compared with any other grease that we knew. 'Treadies' consisted of a cigarette packet filled with the stuff and placed on the floor. The unsuspecting target would tread on it, and it would take forever to remove the stuff from the sole of his shoe. Even better were 'chuckies,' a similar trick where a cigarette carton would be coated with grease on the outside and skilfully thrown so that it attached itself to the ceiling. The ambient warmth of the shop would allow the carton to slowly descend to the floor leaving a cobweb of the vile grease waiting to entrap an unwary passerby. Constant vigilance was another skill that had to be learned!

Then there was the poor fellow whose job it was to fill the oil tanks at the end of the assembly line. The workers meddled with the valve on the pump to ensure that he received a regular shower of oil. He never did understand why it happened, and instead accepted it as part of the job, wearing an oilskin hat and makeshift cape to protect himself, like a refugee from the lifeboat service. The poor cleaner probably suffered most as rubbish was systematically thrown onto the floor where he had just swept. Unfortunately, his anger only prompted the perpetrators to do more of the same. It was childish and inexcusable in retrospect, but that was the way it was.

As apprentices, we were obviously at the receiving end of many jokes, but we had a great deal of fun of our own. We were growing up as well as learning and this meant discovering how to drink and to find our limits of intoxication. Any excuse, birthday, Christmas, or just because it was Friday, was used to visit our local pub, and the gatherings were always fun and never excessive. Darts was our favourite competition.

In those days, attitudes towards drinking and driving were far more relaxed, of course, but even so, in spite of the lax regulations, I had always been taught to be particularly responsible in this regard. On the last day before Christmas, therefore, I left my motorized transport at home so that for once there would be no limitation to our lunchtime excesses. The factory closed at lunchtime, and we walked up the hill to the pub. After a suitably enjoyable time we left and I walked back to catch the bus home.

Desperate by now to relieve myself, I anticipated a brief stop at the factory on the way for that purpose. The place was still open, of course, but I had not anticipated the officious attitude of the gatekeeper on security duty. There was no way that he was going to allow anyone back into a factory with all that dangerous machinery once they had been drinking, and I could not persuade him otherwise.

This was the day that I fully appreciated the advantages of having your own transport, and being able to stop when you wanted to. By the time the bus reached Charlton, I was bursting, and, seeing a public toilet from the top deck of the bus, I rushed to alight from the moving platform. It was a long wait for another bus and it took me the rest of the day to get home. Was the drinking really worth it? I thought not.

Capstan operator 'Mogs' Morgan Drewell with apprentices Bill Cakebread, Mick Odell, Mick Giddings and Denis Boney enjoy a break on the roof. (Courtesy M J Odell)

Hugh Viney had set the tone and spirit of fun in the place from the very top by famously once climbing one of the stone staircases to the roof on a trials bike. Another trials enthusiast had once ridden his bike along the narrow parapet of the roof outside the guard rails, happily without incident, as an error would surely have been fatal.

Jimmy Rudd (right) shares his knowledge of 'Jampot' suspension units with apprentices Terry Wetherfield, Denis Boney, Mick Odell and two other colleagues.

Motorcycle Apprentice

These drawings of the factory layout are based on the collective recollections of those who worked there at the time. They are not to scale, and departments were re-located from time-to-time over the years. (All drawings by G E Josey)

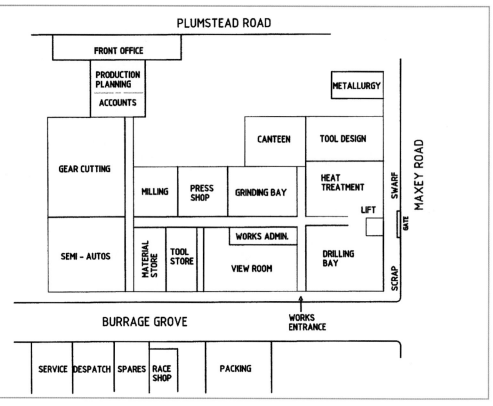

Factory layout – ground floor.

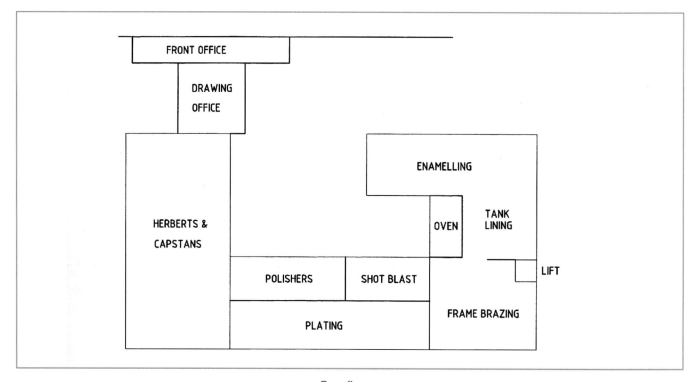

First floor.

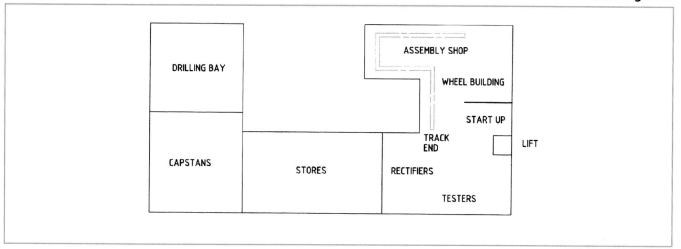

Second floor.

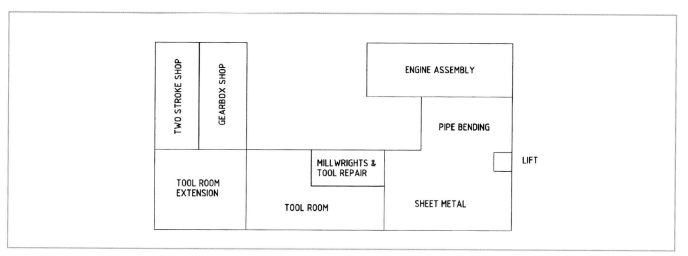

Third floor.

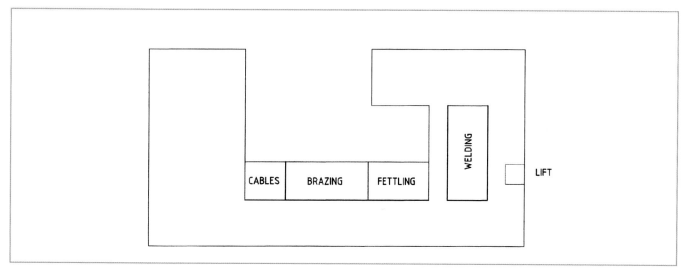

Roof shops.

Motorcycle Apprentice

The roof area was always a magnet as a place for relaxation in the (relatively) fresh air away from the gloom of the factory. To the west, the factory had been extended to house the new machinery with gear-cutting and semi-automatic lathes on the ground floor, and Herbert and capstan lathes on the first floor. More capstans and another Drilling Shop occupied the second floor, with the Tool Room extension and Gearbox Shop above. This area, beyond the Roof Shop building and above the new extension, was fairly uncluttered, and made a useful area for ball games. Unfortunately, these were sometimes a bit extreme, and at one time all staff were banned from the area when a few employees decided to have a game of football using the spherical steel weight from a fly-press as a ball (they can be a tough lot, these motorcyclists!). The 'ball' eventually bounced over the low parapet and between the guard rails to land on the roof of the adjacent single-storey office building. There, it passed through a glass skylight before burying itself, like a cannonball, in the centre of a desk. Happily, as it was lunchtime, the desk was unoccupied, and there were no injuries. It was, however, a salutary awakening to the potential danger of such games.

The area alongside the Roof Shop was used to store castings while they 'weathered' and as a temporary store for unfinished bikes. Occasionally, there would be a shortage of some component, but stopping the production process was costly. To avoid stopping the assembly line, if a bike could be completed so that it was capable of being wheeled away, then production continued leaving the fault to be rectified later. The observant reader will note that the batch of 'lightweight' singles in the photograph (top of page 45) is missing the petrol caps.

The Race Shop was another place that was a magnet for jokers. Isolated from the main factory building as it was, it was for the most part hidden from the all-seeing eyes of the general works management. The type of people that racing attracted also meant that, almost by definition, they were the more adventurous and risk-taking personalities who enjoyed adding a little spice to the working day. The variety of jokes and stunts were numerous, and the revenge attacks were usually worse. I will save some for later.

10 The machine shops

After the initial shock of the Drilling Shop, and the confidence building experience of the Heat Treatment Department, everything else followed with relative ease. That's not to say that I always found it easy to acquire the necessary skills in each department. That would be far from the truth, but I did settle down to enjoy my apprenticeship and always loved the atmosphere and enthusiasm that abounded in the place. Apart from the sheer joy of being involved in the manufacture of motorcycles, AMC was a wonderful place to have an apprenticeship. Other than foundry work, just about every automotive discipline was carried out there, and the factory was very well equipped.

This was particularly true of the general machine shops. At the time, I had accepted the rows of relatively modern machine tools as being the norm for any modern production plant, but many an apprentice must have served his time on much more ancient machinery than that which I was privileged to use.

Later on, I was to discover that, during the five years immediately prior to the start of my employment, Alfred Herbert Ltd., of Coventry had been appointed to totally re-equip the plant with new machine tools. This had been a major investment involving the purchase of nearly 500 new machines, including 150 capstan lathes and 250 drilling spindles/automatics. Apparently, the brief was for the capability to produce 400 engines and 650 gearboxes per week, but production of motorcycles rarely reached those dizzy heights. The Herbert Organization was justifiably proud of its work and its technical journal *Machine Tool Review* produced an excellent twelve page article describing the installation in 1958. The article gives a good insight, not only into the general conditions in the machine shops, but also into the nature of the machining practices involved in the making of a motorcycle. For this reason, it is produced here, in full, for the reader's appreciation.

Overleaf: Alfred Herbert reprint.
(Courtesy BSA Machine Tools)

ASSOCIATED MOTOR CYCLES LTD. PLUMSTEAD ROAD, LONDON, S.E.18

Reprinted from the "Machine-Tool Review", the technical journal published by Alfred Herbert Ltd., Coventry

THIS Company, as the name implies, is an association of five well-known motor cycle manufacturers—Matchless, A.J.S., Norton, Francis Barnett and James. The parent company made the Matchless products—cycles in 1878, the first motor cycle in 1900. In 1931 the Matchless Company acquired the A.J.S. concern, and within a few years the company changed its name to our title which, in recent years, embraced the activities of the three other companies.

The aim of the Associated Company is to produce a range of motor cycles in quantities and at highly competitive prices mainly for the overseas markets; they have been very successful. This joint effort, required for economical reasons, has a centralised production shop at Plumstead in London to augment the individual assembly, sales and service facilities which are still retained at the existing premises of each concern. Matchless and A.J.S. at Plumstead, Norton and James at Birmingham and Francis Barnett at Coventry.

The design and erection of each of the makes of motor cycles has been retained by the respective firms. Standardisation has, however, been adopted as much as possible. A gearbox and a 2½ h.p. 4-stroke engine, for instance, are common to most makers' products. A 2-stroke engine is used for certain models of the James and Francis Barnett range of machines.

Thus we have some of Britain's leading experts in the motor cycle world associated to produce—as is being accomplished—the world's finest and most reliable range of motor cycles.

Fig. 1. Some of the 230 Herbert Drilling Machine Spindles in the Plumstead Works of the Associated Motor Cycles Ltd.

The Association has also permitted large capital expenditure both on the extension of the buildings and in the re-equipping of the machine shops at Plumstead. It is estimated that nearly a million pounds has been spent on the project. New equipment required the expenditure of hundreds of thousands of pounds.

This expenditure was necessary to increase production of a 4-stroke engine, to design and manufacture a 2-stroke engine and a new type gearbox for both types of machine. Prior to the association of the companies, the 2-stroke engines and gearboxes were purchased from other companies.

The Herbert Organisation was virtually appointed as consultants for the whole production project and worked in close co-operation with the production engineers of the Association. The capital expenditure involved was for complete plant and equipment for the production of some 400 engines and 650 gearboxes per week.

During the last five years we have supplied to this Company nearly five hundred machines including 150 Herbert Capstan Lathes, from the smallest to the largest, some 230 Herbert Drilling Machine Spindles and Herbert Auto-Lathes, Milling Machines and Flash Tappers. The Factored Division has supplied several batteries of Archdale Vertical and Horizontal Milling Machines of various capacities, and Brown & Ward Single-spindle Bar Automatics. Other machines included the Cri-Dan High-speed Threading Machine, Archdale Vertical Drilling and Boring Machines, and every conceivable type of machine tool expected to be seen in highly productive and efficient machine shops. The jigs, fixtures and tooling to give the necessary efficiency of production were also supplied.

The accompanying illustrations give a brief indication of the extent of the installation of Herbert-manufactured machine tools.

Apart from the Autos mentioned and twenty other Single- and Multi-spindle Bar Automatics, the whole plant is equipped

Fig. 2. One section of the lathe department which has 29 Herbert No. 2D Capstan Lathes primarily equipped for chuck work up to 9" swing and adequately tooled to perform the maximum number of operations possible in one set-up.

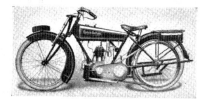

Fig. 3. Early models. (Left) The pioneers with the first A.J.S. machine. (Centre) A 1902 Matchless on the London to Brighton run. (Right) Francis Barnett 1920 "Fanny B".

with the general-purpose type of machines, installed for flow production methods. Handling is reduced to the minimum by grouping different types of machines for the production of a component and its mating parts (see Fig. 9). Machines are also grouped and tooled to produce parts of similar design ; thus, tool-setting, storing and servicing are simplified (see Fig. 22).

It is, however, in the drilling and lathe departments that reductions in production costs have been most marked. Modern machines and efficient tooling permit the adoption of the high production techniques made possible by the design features of both machines and tools. Productivity is mainly dependent on the efficiency of the tooling arrangement—the machine provides the power, rigidity and facilities to use the tooling designed for rapid metal removal consistent with concentricity and good surface finish in the work.

The adaptability of the Herbert Capstan Lathes for techniques requiring rapid production of batches up to medium quantities is well-known. They are designed to ensure maximum efficiency with such methods, although they have proved equally economical on very small batches, six to twelve off, and for continuous production techniques. Herbert Lathes are the simplest to operate and set-up, and have the power, rigidity, alignments and wide ranges of speeds and feeds to meet the varying conditions involved in the machining of materials ranging from light alloys to stainless steels, from heavy roughing to light precision finishing opera-

tions. They can be equipped to minimise the number of operations necessary to machine completely a specific component.

Even though drilling and its associated operations are of a straightforward nature and may not appear to offer much opportunity for reducing machining costs, the results obtained by using new machines and equipment is surprising. This is exemplified in the drilling department at Plumstead. Attention is drawn to :—

(a) the "milling operation" shown in Fig. 25.

(b) the drill depth indicators of Herbert and A.M.C. design fitted to practically all the Herbert Drilling Machines.

(c) the extensive use of the Herbert Quick-change Drill Chuck which virtually converts a single-spindle into a multi-column machine (see Figs. 9 and 19). The drill, the countersinking or radiusing tool, the reamer, the spotfacing tool, can all be interchanged without stopping the spindle and with perfect safety. No spanner, key or tightening is necessary.
The chuck can be integral with the spindle where it is desirable to reduce overhang.

(d) Multi-spindle machines with simple sliding locating fixture (see Figs. 16 and 24).

(e) work locating jigs providing several approaches to the component (see Fig. 19).

(f) Automatic reversing tapping attachments. On a type C machine up to

15 holes can be tapped per minute. It is suitable for right- or left-hand tapping and does not interfere with normal drilling. A small diehead can also be fitted for cutting external threads. If a higher tapping rate is required, the Herbert Flash Tapper, which can be reversed up to 30 times per minute, is used.

(g) Automatic spindle feeds, trips and return traverse, which enable the operator to unload and load on one spindle whilst drilling takes place on another. The pre-selection of a controlled constant feed rate also assists in ensuring long tool life.

(h) The finger-tip control of instantaneous starting, stopping and reversing of the spindle, have also reduced idle time to the minimum. Speed and feed selection is also very simple. These features are necessary to maintain the higher productivity obtained by using the Quick-change Drill Chuck.

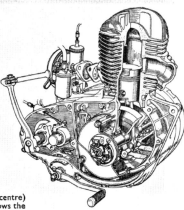

Fig. 4. The 1958 models of the Matchless (left), A.J.S. (centre) and Francis Barnett (right). The sectional drawing shows the compact power unit now built in large quantities in the Plumstead Works of the Associated Motor Cycles Ltd.

Fig. 5. Another section of the Lathe department showing some of the 35 Herbert No. 4 Senior Capstan Lathes installed. The small illustration below shows the latest type Herbert No. 4 Senior Preoptive Capstan Lathe machining wheel hubs in the Norton Works at Birmingham.

Fig. 6. Three photographs taken in the Plumstead Works showing :—

D930. A battery of Archdale Vertical Milling Machines and, at the far end, Herbert Drilling Machines.

D929. A row of Herbert No. 4 Senior Capstan Lathes set up for machining various aluminium cases. Some of the set-ups are shown in Figs. 7, 8 and 24.

D928. Two column- and one bench-mounted Herbert Utility Heads in the Plumstead Works. These heads are extensively used in the fitting shops and assembly lines of many firms. Excellent time-saving devices they enable small components to be polished, reduced in diameter or length, or burrs to be removed without having to return them to the machine shop. They are fitted with a 3-jaw chuck.

4   ASSOCIATED MOTOR CYCLES LTD.

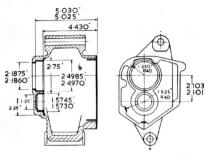

Fig. 7.   Machining gearbox shells on a Herbert No. 4 Senior Capstan Lathe.   Made from aluminium diecastings, the shells have previously been straddle-milled on the lugs and drilled.

The lathe has no square turret on the cross slide and a 2-position indexing work-holding fixture is bolted directly to the spindle flange.   Location is taken from the drilled holes and lugs.

The sequence of operations is as follows :—

    Face end with Ardoloy tool on rear toolpost of cross slide.
    Simultaneously rough bore 2·1875″ and 2·4985″ diameters and 1·250″ radius.
    Simultaneously face the 2·4985″ and 2·75″ diameters.
    Size-bore 2·1875″ and 2·4985″ diameters using Microbore Tools.
    Index fixture.
    Simultaneously bore the 1·25″ diameter, form the bottom face and flat face the 2·25″ diameter.
    Simultaneously rough bore the 1·5745″ diameter, remove sharp edge and bore the 1·625″ radius.
    Size-bore the 1·5745″ diameter using a Microbore Tool.

A single speed of 621 r.p.m. and hand and automatic feeds of 180 (rough bore) and 240 (size bore) cuts per inch are used.   Automatic feed of 180 cuts per inch is also applied to the cross slide in machining the end face.

The floor-to-floor time, 6 minutes.

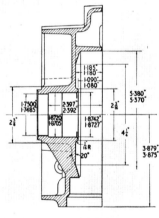

Fig. 8.   Machining the flywheel and bearing housings in the timing side of the crankcase on a Herbert No. 4 Senior Capstan Lathe.   A full complement of tools is held on the turret, all held in substantial tool blocks in knee turning tool holders to ensure maximum rigidity, sustained by the machine and overhead support steady, for cutting with multi-tooling.   The crankcase is gripped on the 2⅝″ diameter boss in a Herbert air-operated chuck.   Tooling on the first turret face faces the 2⅜″ diameter boss, rough bores the flywheel housing (5·380/5·370″ diameter), forms the 20° angle and faces to the 2⅜″ diameter boss.   From the second turret face tooling rough bores the 1·7500″ and 1·8720″ diameters and chamfers the mouth of the flywheel housing.   Simultaneous with this operation, tools in the rear toolpost on the cross slide rough and finish machine the joint face.   Microbore tools on the third turret face size bore the 1·7500/1·7485″ diameter and chamfer the 1·8742/1·8727″ diameter.   Microbore tools are also used to size the 1·8720/1·8705″ and 1·8742/1·8727″ diameters from the fourth and sixth face of the turret respectively.   The operation is completed by size boring the flywheel housing to 5·380/5·370″ diameter, again using the Microbore unit.

The floor-to-floor time is 8 minutes.

All tooling, including the Microbore units, are tipped with Ardoloy which ensures good surface finish and long life between regrinds.

Motorcycle Apprentice

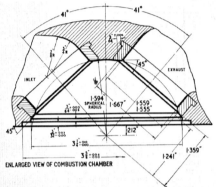

ENLARGED VIEW OF COMBUSTION CHAMBER

Fig. 9. Eleven Herbert Drilling Machines and a Herbert No. 4 Capstan Lathe are grouped to provide line-production machining of cylinder heads. The sequence of operations is as follows :

2. Mill the valve head joint face.

3. Skim cylinder joint face.

4. Drill 18 holes, from $\frac{3}{32}''$ to $\frac{7}{8}''$ diameter, tap 4 holes, ream 2 holes and counterbore 1 hole.

5. (See bottom illustration). Machine the joint face, rough and finish machine the internal spherical dome (1·594 radius), bore the piston clearance and form the 45° chamfer. Special profiling attachments are used on a Herbert No. 4 Capstan Lathe for rough and finish machining the internal spherical dome. The cutting tool is mounted in pivoting jaws actuated by a pusher in the square toolpost on the cross slide which is automatically fed transversely. Spring action reverses the movement of the cutter when the turret is withdrawn and the cross slide movement reversed.

6. Finish drill two $\frac{13}{32}''$ dia. bolt holes.

7. (See centre illustration). Form the valve guide relief in the inlet port, drill four $\frac{19}{64}''$ dia. holes, form taper in the inlet valve throat, form radius in the inlet valve throat, form the exhaust valve throat, bore the valve guide holes, ream the valve guide holes, and form the valve seats. A simple work locating indexing fixture and Herbert Quick-change Drill Chuck for rapid changing of the different tools, reduce idle time. Some of the tools have extensions for piloting in a support bush in the work-holding fixture. All tools are supported at the approach end.

8. Tap nine $\frac{5}{16}''$ 22 t.p.i. × $\frac{1}{2}''$ long holes and counterbore tappet-tube recess.

9. Finish tap nine $\frac{5}{16}''$ 22 t.p.i. holes.

10. Face the valve guide holes.

11. Drill the valve-spring seat locating holes.

12. Drill a $\frac{1}{8}''$ dia. × $4\frac{3}{8}''$ long oil hole through to inlet valve guide hole, open out this hole with No. 3 drill to depth of $\frac{3}{4}''$, spot face, counterbore and tap $\frac{1}{4}''$ 26 t.p.i. to depth of $\frac{1}{2}''$.

13. Drill the exhaust valve guide oil hole.

14. Mill the carburettor flange.

15. Drill and bore the $1\frac{3}{16}''$ guide bush.

16. Open out the inlet port to $1\frac{3}{16}''$ dia. and drill, tap and counterbore two $\frac{5}{16}''$ B.S.F. holes in the carburettor flange.

17. Drill, spot-face, counterbore and tap the sparking plug hole.

18. Bore and spot-face the exhaust port outlet.

6   ASSOCIATED MOTOR CYCLES LTD.

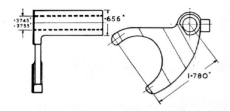

Fig. 10. Machining a selector fork from a steel stamping on a Herbert No. 2D Capstan Lathe fitted with a Herbert 6″ 3-jaw chuck provided with a work support block and two balance weights. The chuck sector-plate screw holes are used for securing purposes. The component is gripped on the ·656″ diameter, the stem locating endwise against the face of a jaw and the prongs of the fork locating on spring-loaded pins held in the support block. The drive to the work is provided by the chuck jaw contacting the boss on the stem.

The operation commences with centring the stem and drilling a ·375″ hole from the solid. The face of the fork is then machined and the ·3745/·3755″ diameter is finish machined and size reamed.

Two spindle speeds are used—455 r.p.m. for all operations except reaming, which is done at a speed of 175 r.p.m. Hand feeds for centring and drilling and automatic feeds of 160 (facing) and 80 (reaming) cuts per inch are used.

Floor-to-floor time, 3½ minutes.

Fig. 11. (Centre illustration). Machining the cast-iron cylinder barrel on a Herbert No. 4 Capstan Lathe. The cast spigot on the cylinder head joint face of the barrel is gripped in a Coventry 3-jaw Chuck. The operation includes rough boring the cylinder barrel to a depth of 3⅜″, rough and finish turning the 2⅞″ and 3⅛″ diameters and, whilst supporting the barrel with a revolving steady, rough and finish machine the face of the spigot relief and chamfer the mouth of the bore.

The tools for finish machining the 50° chamfer, the cylinder bore and finishing the 2⅞″ and 3⅛″ diameters are held in boring bars provided with a pilot which is supported in a steady bush inserted in the chuck bore and with a revolving steady which supports the barrel.

The cylinder barrel is subsequently finish bored to 2·598 ± ·0005″ dia. × 5″ long.

The floor-to-floor time is 8·5 minutes.

Fig. 12. On a Herbert No. 4 Capstan Lathe two sets of cluster tooling mounted in knee turning tool-holders, rough and finish machine the external and internal diameters, and the face of the exhaust port. A recessing tool slide on the turret is used to form a 2″ ± ·005″ dia. × ¼″ recess behind the 2⅛″ threaded diameter. The 2⅛″ × 16 t.p.i. thread is chased from the square turret using the Barson rapid chasing attachment which permits internal or external threading up to a shoulder at high rates of production. The movement of the tool is automatically arrested from the turret and is not dependent on the vigilance of the operator, thus high speeds can be used. The telescopic connection between the chasing holder and turret is removed after the chasing operation.

Floor-to-floor time, 9 minutes.

Fig. 13. Wherever conditions are favourable, Herbert Auto-Lathes are installed in the Plumstead Works to provide the greatest output per foot of floor space at lowest labour cost per piece. A row of No. 3A's is shown below. Machining a rear brake drum from a malleable-iron casting on a Herbert No. 3A Auto Lathe is shown above.

Each face of the turret is fitted with a combination tool-holder for holding a piloted boring bar and toolholders for : (1st turret face), rough turn the outside and $7\frac{11}{32}''$ diameters, rough face the boss and rough bore the $1\frac{3}{8}''$ diameter ; (2nd turret face), finish turn the $7\frac{11}{32}''$ diameter and rough bore the 2·047 and $2\frac{1}{2}''$ diameters (during this operation the side faces of the tooth blank and $6\frac{1}{2}''$ diameter clearance are machined from the rear cross slide) ; (3rd turret face), finish turn outside diameter, finish face the boss and finish bore the $1\frac{3}{8}''$ and $2\frac{1}{4}''$ diameters. Simultaneously with forming the radii on the tooth blank from the front cross slide (4th turret face). Finish bore and chamfer the 2·0470/2·0455″ diameter and chamfer the $2\frac{1}{4}''$ diameter.

Floor-to-floor time, 9 minutes.

Fig. 14. Cluster tooling on three of the turret faces and a facing tool on both the front and rear cross slides on a Herbert No. 4 Auto-Lathe, machine the timing side of the aluminium-alloy diecasting crankcase, as indicated by the heavy lines on the drawing. Rough, semi-finish and finish cuts on the $1\frac{5}{8}''$ and 2·998/2·997 bores, rough and finish cuts on the joint face and $8\frac{1}{2}''$ diameter are taken. Tooling on the turret also removes all sharp corners, machines the $2\frac{5}{8}''$ diameter recess and faces the $3\frac{3}{4}''$ diameter. The boring bars are piloted by a steady bush in the work-holding fixture bore.

Floor-to-floor time, 7 minutes.

8 ASSOCIATED MOTOR CYCLES LTD.

Fig. 15 (above). Precision machining the ball radii in top and bottom races on a Herbert No. 2D Capstan Lathe. The operation includes facing to remove the parting-off burr and rough, semi- and finish-machining the radius. The operator inspects the pitch diameter with the dial gauge shown.

The cutting tools are clamped in substantial holders, held on knee turning tool-holders on the turret provided with overhead support steadies. The tool-holders are of the light-metal type to reduce weight on the turret indexing mechanism and operational fatigue on operations of short duration but requiring continual turret indexing.

The floor-to-floor time for the operation is 1·1 minutes.

The gauge has three locating balls, two are fixed and the other is spring-loaded against an anvil contacting the moving plunger of the dial indicator. Rotating the race in contact with the locating balls indicates any error in pitch diameter.

Fig. 16. Two top columns of Herbert Type M Multi-spindle Drilling Machines mounted on a four-spindle base for drilling and countersinking four ³³⁄₆₄″ diameter holes in the cylinder barrel flange and four ⅜″ B.S.F. tapped holes, 1·063/1·031″ deep, in the cylinder head joint face. The quick-acting, sliding fixtures are located against a back stop.

Floor-to-floor time, 2 minutes.

Fig. 17. In the foreground of the top illustration are two of a forest of Herbert Single-spindle Drilling Machines equipped for two operations on a motor cycle handlebar lug. Holes up to 1¼″ diameter are drilled from the solid, counterbored, spot-faced and reamed. Simple indexing fixtures speed up machining. The wide ranges of speeds and feeds available are of great value in these operations.

In the lower illustration, a Herbert Type C Drilling Machine is efficiently used for performing fifteen different operations—drilling, reaming, tapping, spot-facing and counterboring—on an aluminium outer cover. The Quick-change Drill Chuck has proved a great time saver and the ease of speed and feed changing has reduced operational fatigue in an operation which is performed in 13 minutes.

Motorcycle Apprentice

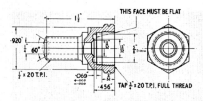

Fig. 18. Efficient, rigid tooling on a Herbert No. 2D Capstan Lathe performing the second operation on a shock absorber bolt produced from a nickel-chrome molybdenum hexagon bar, ·920″ across flats. The operation includes gripping on the ·920″ diameter in a Herbert air-operated 3-jaw chuck, centring, drilling and forming countersink, bottoming with flat drill, forming the ⅜″ diameter recess, boring the thread diameter, facing to ensure ·069″ length, tapping the ⅜″ × 20 t.p.i. thread and finish bore the thread diameter.

Floor-to-floor time, 2 minutes.

Fig. 19. The two principal operations on the front fork slider machined from an alloy diecasting. The set-up on the Herbert No. 4 Capstan turns the 2″ diameter to a length of 1 1/16″, machines the front face, bores the 1¾″ and the long 1 9/16″ diameters and taps the 1 13/16″ × 24 t.p.i. thread.

Rough and finishing cuts are taken on the 1¾″ diameter using piloted cutters, and three cuts—rough and finish boring and reaming—on the 1 9/16″ diameter. The tools for the latter operation are interchanged after successive cuts, thus enabling the operation to be completed in one set-up. The handle A assists in rapid clamping of the boring bars and the reamer.

The floor-to-floor time is 11 minutes.

The drawing shows some of the holes drilled, spot-faced, countersunk, tapped and/or reamed, whilst the slider is held in a simple turnover fixture, on a Herbert three-spindle Drilling Machine. Cutting tools are changed on two spindles, taking advantage of the quick-change chuck. Drill and other tool guides are inserted in four faces of the work holding fixture. The operation, including loading and unloading, takes 6 minutes.

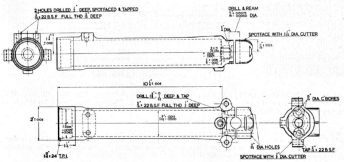

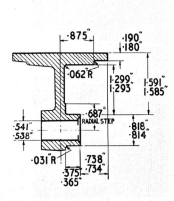

Fig. 20 (above). A cam segment is gripped in a Herbert 9″ air-operated 3-jaw chuck on to which has been bolted support blocks, balance weight and adjusting screw for axial location, for its machining on a Herbert No. 4 Senior Capstan Lathe. The sequence of operations is as follows :—

Centre drill ; simultaneously drill through and rough turn the ·818″ boss ; rough turn the outside diameter from the rear toolpost simultaneously with rough boring the two internal radii from the turret ; rough and finish face the rim and boss ; finish bore the two internal radii and chamfer mouth of the ·541″ bore ; using tools in the square turret face the web, traversing from the ·687″ radial step towards the internal radii and face from the radial step to obtain the ·375/·365″ dimension, simultaneously finish turn the boss to ·814/·818″ diameter, semi-finish and chamfer the ·541/·538″ bore with Microbore tools held in the turret and chamfer both edges of the rim ; the ·541/·538″ diameter is sized with a Coventry Adjustable Reamer.

The floor-to-floor time, 10 minutes.

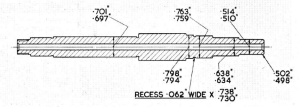

Fig. 21. The tooling (2nd operation) on a Herbert No. 2D Capstan Lathe for turning five diameters, recessing, facing, centring and drilling halfway a gearbox mainshaft. Produced from 1″ diameter bright-drawn steel bar, EN.351, the mainshaft is gripped on the ·701/·697″ diameter in a hand-operated dead-length bar chuck locating against the shoulder of the outside diameter. The ·638″ and ·763″ diameters are turned in one cut, by Chipstream Boxtools on the turret at a spindle speed of 695 r.p.m. and automatic feed of 320 cuts per inch ; the shaft is supported by a live centre after centre drilling, whilst the ·798″ and ·514″ diameters and the recess are formed with tools held on the two toolposts on the rear of the cross slide. A parallel shank drill of special length drills a $\frac{19}{32}$″ diameter hole from the solid to a length of $4\frac{3}{8}$″ with a spindle speed of 930 r.p.m. and hand feed.

Floor-to-floor time, 4½ minutes.

Ardoloy-tipped tools are used throughout and it will be seen that the Chipstream Boxtool is fitted with a chip deflector which diverts the long coiled turning produced into the tray of the machine. The Chiprupter fitted to the machine enables these turnings to be broken into convenient lengths for disposal whilst cutting is in progress.

Motorcycle Apprentice

Fig. 22. At the Plumstead Works of the Associated Motor Cycles Co., two Herbert No. 4 Senior Capstan Lathes are permanently tooled for performing the two major operations on each of the front and rear hub shells. Machined from aluminium-alloy diecastings with a cast-in malleable-iron brake liner, the first operation is on the brake liner side (see D.934), the machined faces of which are used in the 2nd operation for location against studs bolted to the sector plate of the Coventry Chuck, and the faces of the three special chuck jaws. The heavy lines on the drawing indicate the surfaces machined in the 2nd operation on the rear hub shell with the set-up shown at D.933. As with all set-ups at these works, tooling is substantial—large diameter fluted boring bars with detachable multi-edged boring cutters, and adjustable floating reamers for precision machining the 1·749/1·748″ diameter. Apart from the overhead support feature, extra support is provided by a live centre locating in the bore of the shell, when the outside diameter and radius are formed from the cross slide.

The floor-to-floor time for this operation is 10 minutes.

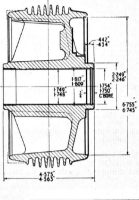

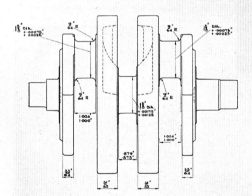

Fig. 23. An unusual vertical turret mounted on the front of the cross slide of a Herbert No. 4 Capstan Lathe, set-up for machining crankshafts. The main bearing and crankpin diameters and widths of the shrouds on single- and twin-throw crankshafts can be machined with this equipment ; the chucking arrangement differs to locate either the axis of the crankpin or bearing in line with the machining axis. The illustrations show the machining of the shrouds and crankpin of a two-throw crankshaft which is set on the machine, to the crankpin axis. The front face is machined and centred, after which a live centre in the turret supports the shaft whilst the faces between the shrouds and the $1\frac{1}{8}$″ crankpin diameter and $\frac{9}{64}$″ radii are machined.

The widths of the Ardoloy-tipped cutter blades are of a size to permit roughing and finishing cuts to produce the 1·004/1·000″ and $1\frac{1}{8}$″ + ·00075/+ ·00025″ dimensions.

After machining, the crankshaft is reversed to repeat the operation on the other crankpin and shroud faces.

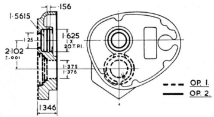

Fig. 24. The 2nd operation on a gearbox inner cover using a Herbert No. 4 Senior Capstan Lathe fitted with a hand-operated fixture bolted to the spindle flange. The aluminium-alloy diecasting is located on a plug by a previously reamed 1⅜″ diameter hole and radially, on the profile, between clamping and adjusting screws.

The sequence of operations is simultaneously bore the 1·25″ and 1·5615″ diameters and counterbore the threaded diameter ; simultaneously face the bottom of the 1·5615″ diameter, form the ·156″ wide recess and chamfer the mouth of bore ; size-bore the 1·5615″ diameter, using Microbore Unit, and tap the 1⅝″ × 20 t.p.i. thread with Herbert Ground Thread Tap.

Machine the front joint face.

A spindle speed of 1,000 r.p.m. (tapping 40 r.p.m.) and either hand or automatic feed (tapping, size boring and facing) of 240 cuts per inch are used.

The floor-to-floor time, 5½ minutes.

The illustration on the left shows the three Herbert Type M Multi-drill top columns mounted on a common base for drilling seven ·328″ diameter holes and drilling and tapping five ¼″ diameter 26 t.p.i. holes in the gearbox inner cover. The cover is clamped in a single fixture which is located by a back rail and fingers as it is moved from one operating position to the next. Floor-to-floor time for complete operation is 3 minutes.

Fig. 25 (right). The operator is shown using a Herbert Single-spindle Type C Drilling Machine equipped with a work holding fixture and jig for drilling four ⅛″ diameter oil holes in the timing side of the crankcase. The standard machine table has been removed to increase the vertical capacity of the machine and the drill depth indicator, of A.M.C.'s own design, assists in drilling to close limits on depth. A drill steady is bolted to the bottom column of the machine and drill guide bushes are inserted in the cross plate.

When the crankcase halves are assembled, a 1⅛″ radius is milled the full width of the case to accommodate the dynamo in the power unit. This operation is also shown. Two complete crankcases are milled simultaneously ; the cases are located radially on pegs fitted to the fixture which is also provided with a steady bush to pilot the milling cutter spindle as the cutter is fed down to remove approximately 3/32″ of metal.

The former operation is done in 3·5 minutes, the latter in 1·33 minutes.

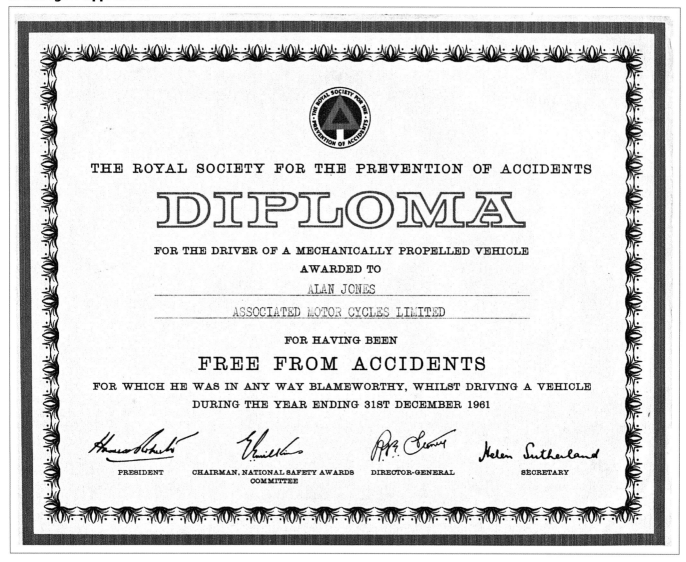

A tester's well-earned safety certificate. (Courtesy A Jones)

The abiding memory that attaches itself to all of the machine shops is the cutting oil. Overalls and other clothes became soaked in the milky liquid and it permeated the skin so that only a good soak in a hot bath could rid you of the smell. As our house did not have the luxury of a bathroom, baths were restricted to Friday nights only, so one tended to become used to living with cutting oil during the week. Even so, we were luckier than some. Our house did at least have a bath. Many in the area did not. The only problem was that it also served as the base for the only work surface in the kitchen. The bath was blessed with a cold tap only, hot water being produced by a gas fired cylindrical boiler that stood on ornate cast iron legs in the corner. From there, it was ladled in a large saucepan into the bath. Bath nights were, therefore, a major ritual for the whole of the family, and there was no opportunity to be flexible with the

timing. Many houses in south London at the time had no bath facilities whatsoever. Their occupants had no alternative other than a weekly visit to the public baths. In fact, it had been only a few years before I started work at AMC, that our house had been equipped with electric lighting.

The public baths offered an alternative but was an experience in itself. The individual steel-walled cubicles each housed a bath, a slatted wooden seat and enough room to change. The bath was equipped with a single faucet that dispensed both hot and cold water and, apparently for safety reasons, there were no taps. The attendant would, therefore, control the volume and temperature of water required when you entered. Having closed the door and immersed oneself in the water, the temperature was controlled by calling out to the attendant: "More hot in number 12 please." A favourite trick was to call out someone else's cubicle number and listen for the screams as the unexpected hot or cold water arrived! This was the only alternative if, for any reason, you missed your 'slot' on a Friday night. Such were the simple pleasures of bath time.

The oil was at its worst in the Gear-Cutting Department where, instead of the usual lightweight and milky-white cutting oil, something heavier and clearer, more akin to engine lubricating oil, was used. This soaked into the clothes and kept them permanently oil-soaked and heavy. Barrier creams, applied before work each day, kept the worst skin complaints at bay, but anyone who suffered from adolescent spots was destined to keep them for a very long time in that environment.

Associated with the cutting oils was the faint mist that hung in the air in all of the machine shops. If we worried about what our hands were immersed in every day, then we should probably have been doubly worried at what we might be breathing in. Happy in our ignorance, we were oblivious to such thoughts, and the COSH (Control of Substances Hazardous to Health) regulations, which would enhance workers' awareness of the risks that they faced, were unknown to us at the time.

In general, once the basic skills were acquired, work in the machine shops was fairly tedious and boring. The routine for training was to spend a week or two observing various operators, and then be given a machine of one's own to operate. The operations were always repetitive and, as apprentices, there was no opportunity to liven the proceedings by going faster and earning a bonus like your fellow workers. They mostly looked on us as fools who had been conned by the management into working for the pittance that we did. In spite of the ridiculously low rate of pay and the relatively long hours, the need for money still meant that every opportunity to work overtime was readily accepted. The normal hours were 8.00am to 6.00pm, and normal overtime meant 7.00am to 7.00pm, plus 8.00am to 12.00 on Saturday. The rate increased to 'time and a third' for weekday overtime, and 'time and a half' for Saturdays. In theory, there was also 'double time' available for Sunday working, but this opportunity rarely arose for the lowly apprentices.

It was the characters that made the machine shops interesting, workers, chargehands and managers alike, each with their own personal enthusiasms and interests. Some, like my mentor in the Drilling Shop, would spend their time constantly trying to brainwash you with their own brand of politics or religion. Others, like helpful Ray in the Milling Bay, would spend much of his time extolling the virtues of his beloved Lancia, and would patiently try to convert you on the benefits of the 'narrow V-four' engine configuration. It would be many years later before I would come to appreciate the engineering qualities of the motor car that he loved so much.

One of the down sides of working in a motorcycle factory where most of the employees were dedicated riders or competitors, was the high proportion of employees that were physically damaged in some way. It was a way of life and, although they were aware of the risks involved, such was their love of motorcycling, that they still considered the risks to be acceptable. I was proud to be one of them. The testers were most at risk, of course, partly due to the high mileages that they covered,

irrespective of the weather, and partly because sometimes, what they were testing was an experimental prototype and, on occasions, something broke! I remember one tester telling me how a steering head casting fractured at speed, leaving him with the handlebars and all of the controls in his hands but with no connection to the front wheel. To his credit and probably due to his wealth of experience, he managed to bring the machine to a stop without falling off. Another tester held claim to the fact that he had broken every bone in his body during his long employment with the company, but I suspect that his claim was a gross exaggeration of the truth. By contrast, tester Alan Jones had an incredible accident free record, and was presented with a certificate to prove it! Even so, he was also not immune from accidents. One of the benefits to be gained from testers, of course, was the expert feedback that they could provide to the designers. On one such occasion, Alan criticized the poor ground clearance of the exhaust system on the lightweight 250CSR. His criticism was not accepted and so he took the Drawing Office Manager, Tony Denniss, for a ride on the pillion. Some enthusiastic right-hand cornering saw both of them deposited in the road and the exhaust was modified!

Neither should we forget the mental scars. There is a supreme responsibility in the process of designing and manufacturing a vehicle, and there are many components in a motorcycle, the failure of which can be catastrophic and sometimes fatal. To have made a mistake that may have caused such an accident is a heavy responsibility to bear and, during my employment, I witnessed one person carrying such a burden. In that case, I believe the self punishment was misplaced, but that did not remove his suffering from the thought that he just might have been the cause.

It came as something of a surprise, therefore, while spending my time in the Grinding Shop, when a casual discussion about accidents produced a conversation that showed that it was just as dangerous inside the factory as out! I can't recall his name but he was a short, sturdy bloke, no youngster, probably in his early fifties at the time. He was a quiet person who, dressed in an ex-WD trench coat and flat cap, used an olive-green, plunger-sprung BSA Bantam as ride-to-work transport. He was one of the old style motorcyclists like my Father. It must have been in the early stages of my spell in the Grinding Bay as my duties were again restricted to 'watch and learn' and my presence had been forced upon this particular unfortunate. This was always the tedious part, working with a total stranger and enduring forced idleness through the long days. There was little to do but try to make conversation.

Now, this character had a distinctive dent in his skull that rose from above one eyebrow to the top of his forehead. It could be seen from the scar that it was clearly the result of an injury and one day I chanced to ask him if it was the result of another bike accident, as I had never seen him wear a crash-helmet. "No," he replied, "I did it standing here!" He then proceeded to explain how he had been grinding the big-end journals on twin crankshafts. This was done with the pair of big-ends held between centres, with the main bulk of the mainshaft and flywheels running eccentrically, of course. The heavy crankshaft would,

Motorcycle Apprentice

therefore, be seriously out of balance during this operation. On this occasion, he was preparing to grind a new crankshaft but did not locate the centres correctly before starting the operation. When the machine started to spin, the massively out of balance crankshaft was dislodged and flew out of the machine. He was clearly lucky to have survived, but he was still happy to pick up a crankshaft from the floor and demonstrate the perfect fit of the flywheel into the radius formed in his skull!

A spell in the Press Shop was exciting. While my apprenticeship was in progress, the company invested in a new 300 ton (305 tonne) press, so tall that it necessitated the building of a tower in the middle of the factory roof to cover it. It was an impressive piece of equipment, and was mainly used for pressing out petrol tanks and tool boxes, etc. The instant transformation of a plain sheet of steel into a fully formed component was fascinating, but the noise of the assembled presses was something else. Later on, while working in the Tool Room on the press tools themselves, I returned to the big press but cannot say that I was ever comfortable working inside it. No matter what safety measures were in place, the thought of 300 tons sitting above one's head was something that I could never relax about. Towards the end, when the company was in a bad way, it supplemented manufacture by taking in sub-contract work, and the press was used to stamp out 'Mobo' rocking horses!

The spell of circulating the machine shops culminated in another soft job in the 'View Room.' These days it would be called an Inspection or Quality Control Department, but in the 1950s, 'View Rooms' were quite common. I guess that it was terminology left over from the Second World War, and quite reasonably described what was actually the process, i.e. looking at, or 'viewing,' the finished component. The View Room was logically sited adjacent to the Grinding Bay, which was also conveniently close to the main factory entrance for personnel and the canteen. Grinding was usually the last operation for any component following the various stages of machining and heat treatment, etc. It was, therefore, a vulnerable place where parts might go 'missing' before they were consigned to the security of the View Room and Stores.

The office was panelled in glass and well equipped with a wide range of measuring equipment, including air gauges, etc., for measuring cylinder bores. There were also hardness and crack testing facilities. After time spent in the machine shops, however, the work was clean and relatively quiet, and, as a bonus, for the first time, you were also allowed to sit down! The apparently simple skills learned in using measuring equipment effectively should not be underestimated.

In spite of the generally clean and peaceful atmosphere that pervaded in the department, it was here that I was given one of the most physically demanding jobs of the entire five year apprenticeship. It was at the time of the awful change-over from magneto ignition and dynamos to coil ignition and alternators. The change had been fraught with many problems and beset with unreliability. The twin-cylinder machines had used a cast iron crankshaft with a stubby output shaft, and the alternator version now demanded an extended shaft to support the rotor. Presumably, due to a lack of stock of the new crankshafts and a surplus of the old ones, a batch had been modified by manufacturing a short extension shaft. At this point, I think that I should ask the reader not to be shocked, as the method of securing the shaft extension was to screw it into place after being coated with sal-ammoniac solution so that it would be securely rusted in position! For added security, it was cross-pinned with a dowel before the final machining operations were completed, and it appeared to be one solid shaft when finished.

The problem then came when, for whatever reason, perhaps a spares demand, a batch of the old crankshafts was required and there was no stock. A hapless apprentice was, therefore, appointed to reverse the modification. In theory, the process was simply to remove the new extension shaft by unscrewing it. Unfortunately, however, the location of the sturdy cross-pin had been hidden by the final machining operations and the sal-ammoniac had proved to be very effective. The only option was brute force. After clamping a crankshaft in a large vice, a Stilson pipe wrench was used, combined with a long length of steel tube for additional leverage. The cross-pin was sheared in the process and the thread was literally ripped out of the shaft as the bond was destroyed. Of course, the new extension shafts were reduced to scrap in the process but that was of little concern compared to the value of a fully machined crankshaft. My only consolation for the pain was the growth of some new muscles and an unexpected respect for rust as a bonding agent!

11 The jaywalker

The 500cc BSA B33 served me well, taking me through my driving test and introducing me to long distance motorcycling. It also had adequate performance for a novice; more, that is, than my parents would have preferred. It didn't look like the 'Gold Star' B34 that I really wanted, however, as it still had an old-fashioned rigid rear end with no springing, and an incongruous dual-seat that dated it amongst the motorcycles of my peers. A trip to the breaker's yard at Pride and Clarke in Stockwell Road, Brixton one Saturday morning soon sorted that little problem. A plunger-sprung rear frame, complete with 'cush-drive' rear wheel, was a bolt-on kit purchased over the counter for the princely sum of £7-10 shillings (I still have the receipt!). This, together with shiny new alloy mudguards, and some home-made brackets combined with the pattern dual-seat and I had (in my eyes at least) my Gold Star lookalike. To my eternal disgrace, the perfect original rear frame and mudguards - which my father was not slow to point out were much more effective than their replacements - were consigned to the scrapheap. The final 'piece de resistance' was fitting a pair of part-worn racing tyres and tubes, scrounged from the Racing Department.

This, then, was my pride and joy, at least until I could afford something better. It gave me reliable transport to work and a great deal of fun

riding out with my friends Ray (BSA B32) and Dave (now Norton 88-mounted) whose 'featherbed' frame was deeply envied. It all came to grief one wet workday evening ...

It had been a dismal wet day, and it must have been winter as it was very dark when we left work, fully kitted up, for the damp journey home after doing the usual maximum 7.00am to 7.00pm shift. I felt jaded as I pulled out of the company car park, along with an older employee riding a standard and not very new 500cc AJS. We rode in company across the cobbles in Beresford Square and past the policeman on point duty outside the Woolwich Arsenal gates. We then opened our throttles for

The 'improved' B33. The original rigid rear frame and steel mudguards were consigned to the scrapheap. It's enough to make a purist weep.

Motorcycle Apprentice

Former school friend, Dave Jackman, sits outside the house in Bawtree Road. The Dominator 88 that replaced his B31 BSA was deeply envied.

Killing a policeman was a capital offence in those days.

The hot exhaust pipe was burning a hole through my rubber boots when help came to thankfully relieve me from the weight of by battered motorcycle. Strangely, both bus passenger and policeman seemed to have disappeared while I gathered myself together and parked the bike at the roadside. Soon, however, the policeman appeared from the approach to the ferry, gripping the bus passenger by the scruff of the neck.

After politely checking that I was OK and had no broken bones, the policeman then proceeded to give the pedestrian a severe lecture about the stupidity of his actions, threatened to charge him with jay-walking (I had never considered that there could be such an offence) and praised me for my quick thinking reactions in laying the bike down so that I didn't cut him in two (as if I had any option)! He then noted my smashed headlight and asked if I wanted to make a claim against the pedestrian for damages to my bike. In truth, the glass had been cracked a week or two earlier and the rest could be straightened. I just wanted to get away while I still had no charges against me. Damage to the bike had been the least of my worries.

Then, just when I thought that it was over, a helpful gentleman witness came forward. "Yes officer, I saw it all. I was waiting at the bus stop when this mad motorcyclist came racing around the corner with his pillion passenger. I saw them knock you down. I will be your witness." Pillion passenger? What he had seen was obviously the aftermath of the initial collision when I was sliding down the road with the downed bus passenger on top of me! The policeman thanked him kindly and told the 'witness' that his assistance would not be needed, and I breathed another sigh of relief.

As I made ready to leave this unhappy scene, a possible reason for the policeman's understanding became clear. Parked around the corner was his trusty Velocette LE. He was a police motorcyclist on temporary point duty. Seeing the accident unfold from his perfect vantage point, he could easily put himself in my position and could probably sympathize with the difficulty in trying to brake so hard downhill on that slippery surface. He was probably grateful that it was me and not him!

I counted myself lucky. I suffered only minor bruises and a chipped tooth but gained an important lesson in prudence and road-craft. Apart from a few grazes, bent footrest and gear and kick-starter levers, the bike was undamaged and we both quickly recovered.

the stretch of straight road that ends with a left curve before the dip to the crossroads at the Woolwich ferry, where another policeman would be controlling the traffic.

We certainly weren't racing each other, but whenever motorcyclists are riding together there always seems to be a slightly competitive 'edge' to the proceedings. I knew that my fellow rider lived north of the Thames and would, therefore, be turning right onto the ferry. The only challenge, therefore, was to stay in front until then. This I did, but whether this was due to the better accelerative performance of my bike or the wisdom of my more experienced accomplice, I will never know.

We banked gently to the left for the curve by the power station. I didn't know exactly where my colleague from work was, except that he was behind me and was probably now slowing as we approached the ferry. A double-decker London bus was slowing for a bus stop on my left with an exposed platform full of passengers waiting to alight. Before the bus came to a stop, however, a young man jumped from the platform and, without looking behind him, ran diagonally across the road into my path.

He was very close. I brought the bike upright as much as possible and braked hard on the slippery downhill slope, trying to steer to the right in the vain hope that he might see or hear me. In an instant, the front wheel kicked to the left and the bike crashed to the ground. With my right leg trapped under the bike, and my foot wedged between kick-starter and footrest, we hit the bus passenger in the back of the legs. The ground was close to my eyes now as we headed inexorably for the policeman on point duty. Now the policeman also was down. A heap of three people and a motorcycle now lay in the middle of the road junction. My primary thought was waiting for the impact as the following AJS joined the melee, but thankfully it did not come. My second thought was of prison bars as I briefly pondered the possible penalty for knocking down a policeman!

12 Fire in the Assembly Shop

The assembly line – obviously a posed picture as it was never that tidy!
(Courtesy Greenwich Heritage Centre)

that he imagines, being part of a team assembling these immaculate creations. Most motorcyclists would feel that they were in heaven to be there, but my obsession was with the racing bikes and, for that reason, I managed to engineer it so that my stay in Assembly was relatively brief.

The primary interest would be in the production line which was simple enough in its arrangements. A narrow-gauge railway track ran around the walls and then turned sharp right along another short wall that terminated near the lift shaft on the second floor. Each bike was built on a small trolley that ran on these rails. There was no power to the system, and the trolleys were advanced manually from one build station to the next by the assembly staff. Each build station was equipped with storage boxes that would be pre-loaded with components appropriate to that stage of

What a dream of a place the Assembly Shop was! When a young man dreams of working in a motorcycle factory, this is the image the build for the batch of whatever model was being assembled at the time. The motorcycle would start as a bare frame, and

Testers returning to the entrance gate in Maxey Road.
(Courtesy Greenwich Heritage Centre)

A present-day view of the same scene.

Tester Alan Jones has an
unenviable job on an icy
morning.
(Courtesy A Jones)

Alan returns safely to
the factory after what
must have been a nerve-
wracking test ride.
(Courtesy A Jones)

Motorcycle Apprentice

would arrive near the lift shaft completed, where it would be lifted with a small electric hoist and placed onto its wheels.

Somewhere near the termination of the track, the wheels were laced up with what seemed to be amazing speed and dexterity. Forks would arrive at the line as a complete sub-assembly, and engine and gearboxes would similarly be delivered from their respective departments. On the left of the lift shaft was the 'run up' area where the machines would be filled with lubricants and fuel before being started for the first time. They would then be taken on road test, and, following that, would either be approved for dispatch or returned to the 'Rectification Department.' This occupied the floor area on the other side of the lift where any corrective work was completed by a specialist rectifier or the testers themselves. It always seemed slightly odd to me that the production processes started on the ground floor and terminated on the second floor. The lift, with doors at both ends, was manned by a permanent operator for good reason.

For me, personally, the main interest was in the characters themselves, particularly the testers. They were true dyed-in-the-wool motorcyclists, weathered and hardened by the thousands of miles ridden in every season of the year. It was not a very glamorous or easy life, and anyone who thinks only of the joy of being paid to ride new motorcycles every day is a fool indeed. No, this job demanded a real love of motorcycling. To us apprentices they were the gods of the motorcycling world and their riding skills were to be envied. To test an untried motorcycle or put up huge daily mileages in all weathers demanded a unique blend of dedication and skill. In truth, most of us who envied their freedom and the variety of their work on a fine sunny day, would be cowering in fear and trepidation if asked to do their job on a bleak winter morning.

The most spectacular event in the Assembly Shop was on the day of the fire. It occurred in the start-up area where small carburettor fires were not uncommon. A small error in setting the ignition timing, or a very tight engine, made the recipe and the subsequent backfire was all that was needed to start a conflagration. This fire started in just that way. The important thing in any crisis is to keep calm, and most people experienced in this subject know that the simplest and quickest way to put out a carburettor fire is simply to continue and re-start the engine. If you are fortunate, the engine will run and immediately suck in the flames. Drama over. On this occasion, however, this trick was either missed or didn't work. Instead, the employee concerned had thrown a fire blanket over the bike. All seemed to be fine until the blanket was removed. This revealed the bike to be well alight under the blanket, with the flames consuming the seat and wiring harness and licking hungrily around the petrol tank. Panic!

A happy group in the assembly shop: L to R, Eric Pratt, unknown apprentice, Alan Jones, Hugh Coleman, Jimmy King, George Batley, Neil Collet, Arthur Martin, Joe Allen, Johnny Penfold, with Johnny Foster and Sid Werner seated. (Courtesy W Hawkins)

71

Motorcycle Apprentice

The factory was well equipped with fire fighting facilities, etc. and close to hand was a particularly large extinguisher consisting of two cylinders mounted on a two-wheeled trolley. It had its own hose and, once set off, it quickly doused the fire with foam, but then what to do? The extinguisher was clearly designed for much larger fires and was filling the shop with foam! The employee had to do something quickly so he wheeled the extinguisher to the outside wall and poked the hose out of the window. Problem solved! Unfortunately, nothing is ever that simple, and outside, the hose, still emitting generous volumes of foam under pressure, was flailing about like a maddened snake from the second floor window.

As I have said, the start-up area was adjacent to the lift and, therefore, immediately above the stretch of road where the newly finished bikes were lined up with their rear wheels to the kerb awaiting test or dispatch. They were smothered, as were all of the cars within range, those belonging to employees and the neighbouring houses alike. The production line was stopped and all available staff was directed to car and bike cleaning duties until the mess was cleared. I guess that extinguisher was just too much of a good thing and it was an object lesson in when not to use a fire blanket.

13 Homework & theft

A question most frequently asked of me is: "Why, when working for AMC, did you choose to ride a BSA?" Historically, of course, my first bike, the side valve C10, was purchased before I secured my employment, and when it came to the next change, to the B33, BSAs were simply more plentiful and cheaper to buy. This had been the essential deciding factor with the original purchase. It also says something about the BSA when a 16 year old can dismantle and rebuild one without any previous knowledge, and have it then provide several years of reliable transport. They must be very simple and very tough, and probably both.

I must be honest, however, and confess that I never developed a real love for my employer's bread and butter products. Although, undoubtedly built to a higher quality standard than many of their competitors, I still considered them to be, like the BSA, the 'grey porridge' of the industry. Oh yes, I could drool over the 7R and G50 racers and the beloved Porcupine, and even had a soft spot for the trials machines and the occasional G12 CSR when fitted with that minimal competition tank. I think that the basic problem with the single cylinder production was that there was no family connection between the road machines and the racers. The engineering was totally different. The rider of a BSA B31 or B33, or the rider of a Velocette MAC or MSS, could always convince himself that it was like a Gold Star or Viper/Venom, but for a few small (but very important!) details. For the rider of an AMC machine, no such comparison was possible, unless his particular enthusiasm was for trials riding or scrambles. Now, if only they still marketed an overhead-cam machine like the pre-war R7 or R10, then it would have been a totally different story.

With the benefit of the insight gained from my privileged position as an employee, I was, of course, aware of the quality of the AMC production when compared with other makes. The quality of its plating and stove-enamelling was truly second to none. Later experience only served to confirm this view. My real love has always been for Nortons, Velocettes and Vincents. Of these, only the Velocette would I place alongside the AMC products in engineering quality, and, although I still love all three makes dearly, my knowledge and experience has shown that both the Norton and the Vincent could be positively agricultural in their build quality by comparison with the Velocette and the AMC products. It was, therefore, inevitable in some way that the B33 would be part exchanged for an immaculate 1957 Velocette MAC (TUC 574) at Valentine Motors, Bromley. It was in superb condition, and rather suspiciously had been fitted with a brand new petrol tank, suggesting that it had recently been dropped. It was so new, in fact, that when I first saw it, there were no petrol taps fitted, and there was still enamel in the threaded holes where the taps should have been! There were no other signs of damage, however, and it turned out to be a very good buy.

Apart from the occasional Vincent enthusiast and eccentric like me, most of the employees rode the company's products. The reason for this was simple: They cost nothing to maintain. I never saw it written down anywhere but there seemed to be an unwritten law that if you were an employee, loyal to the company's products, then the supply of parts to maintain it would be free. It seemed that whatever you wanted, there was always a departmental manager who would help you to get it, in order to keep you on the road. Apart from spares, chrome and cadmium plating or stove enamelling of anything was readily available. To have your ports gas-flowed or some polishing done might cost you a packet of cigarettes, but little more. The system was, no doubt, abused by some, but in all honesty, if it was, then I didn't see it. There was a story of one group who had been caught lowering baskets of spares down from the roof of the factory to a waiting van. The members of this group were later prosecuted. Such blatant theft deserved its punishment. The company policy was supportive of motorcyclists, and abuse of its generosity in this way was grossly unfair. There were some

The faithful Velocette.

Hugh Viney
in Burrage
Grove.
(Courtesy
Mortons)

serious motorcyclists at the top, including Jock West and Hugh Viney, and this permeated enthusiasm throughout the company. Jock West had been known to take a 7R or G50 (fitted only with trade plates and a bung up the megaphone) for a blast, and Hugh Viney once famously rode his trials bike up the main staircase from the entrance, up the four levels of the factory, and out onto the roof. How many senior managers would do that just for fun?

The manufacturing facilities were good and just about anything could be made and finished to a high standard. There was almost a challenge when someone needed something, and there was little problem getting 'homework' done once you had established friends in the right places. Later in my apprenticeship, I graduated to driving an MG TC that needed a lot of work. In the process of rebuilding it, I needed a new exhaust system but could ill afford one. A new pipe complete with flanges and silencer was made and suitably designed so that it could be taken out past security under my coat and transported home on my bike. Such service! I have no doubt that exhaust system outlasted anything I could have purchased. The Sheet Metal Shop also had a nice sideline in tool boxes. One of the popular standards was a box to house tool-making instruments, somewhere to keep your micrometers, callipers and dividers, etc. They had two slide-out drawers with an open tray above. They could be purchased for a few pounds in the Sheet Metal Shop. Mine, finished in its original black AMC stove enamel, is still doing admirable service in my garage, nearly 50 years later!

All these petty thefts and 'perks' were small fry compared to the great train robbery ... or rather the little van robbery(?) of 1961. Unfortunately, it happened on the day when I was at college, and I missed all of the action.

The works hack was a dark blue sign-painted Ford Thames van used mainly for local deliveries and transporting bikes and spares to the railway station. It was also used to collect the weekly wages from the bank. Wages in those days were still distributed in cash in folding notes and small change, together with your wages slip in a little square brown envelope. (A long brown envelope meant redundancy or something sinister.)

To ensure a quick journey and avoid being delayed in traffic, the route used was through the relatively quiet back streets between the Plumstead Road and the railway line. Two motorcycle outriders (seconded from the testers) followed the van on these trips. They were presumably there as added protection, but they obviously served to advertise to any criminals the fact that the van was carrying something more than just motorcycle parts.

On this occasion, as the van crossed a minor junction in Vincent Road, close to the factory, the criminals forced the van off the road before ramming it with another Ford saloon. The group then attacked and threatened the driver and the outriders with iron bars and smashed the rear window to gain access to the cash.

Unfortunately for the criminals, the £10,000 wages was

The Evening News and Star, Thursday, July 13, 1961   G 9

COSH GANGS GRAB £8,000 PAYROLLS

Cashiers Fight The Masked Raiders

MASKED pay bandits grabbed £8,000 in two raids to-day. At Plumstead six men got away with £3,000 and in another attack at Ramsgate, Kent, a gang of five made off with a £5,000 payroll.

The Plumstead gang, armed with iron bars, waited in two stolen cars and a van for Associ-

The wages van with the back window smashed by the bandits.

ated Motor Cycles' wages van with its two motor-cycle escorts to arrive in Vincent-street, Plumstead.

Then they struck. Fifty-six-year-old Mr. Bert Jenner, of Perton-road, Eltham, one of the motor-cycle escorts, said: "As we drew near the factory a car drew out and forced our van on to the pavement. A second car then rammed it. Six young men sprung out of the cars.

"Two of them pushed me off my machine and one of them wearing a grey nylon stocking mask over his face hit me over the head and shoulder with an iron bar. I fell to the ground dazed."

As the other bandits threatened the van driver, Mr. T. Meehan, the rest of the gang smashed the van's rear window, forced open the door and threatened wages manager, Mr. R. Wilson, and guard, Mr. Walter Pettyfer.

Police believe the bandits thought the van was made to collect the £10,000 wages. But plans had been made to get these on another day.

At Ramsgate five bandits wearing nylon stocking masks smashed down three railway-men in a street near Ramsgate

railway station and grabbed a £5,000 payroll intended for British Railways staff in East Kent.

The cash, mostly in notes, was being taken to the station in a taxi when a van rammed the taxi.

The five bandits tore open the taxi doors and attacking the three men inside.

There followed a terrific fight before the bandits using coshes, got the money.

Mr. Frederick Nicholls, another railway employee, of Newington-road, Ramsgate, saw the battle in the driving mirror of his car.

He said: "I was acting as pilot to the taxi and was about 50 yards ahead of it when the van appeared.

"It drove straight at the taxi and I saw four or five men leap out and surround it. I could see them beating up the occupants and I was just going to their help when one of the bandits came running towards me. I managed to dodge him but his cosh smashed the windscreen.

The bandits escaped in a red and grey Ford Zodiac saloon with the registration letters XLC 346.

When Mr Nicholls reached the taxi he found his three colleagues dazed and bleeding on the floor.

The taxi-driver was not injured.

The bandits used this car to ram the wages van in the pay ambush in Vincent-street, Plumstead, to-day.

Mr. George Batley (left) and Mr. Bert Jenner acted as motor-cycle escorts for the Plumstead firm's wages van.

Newspaper cutting about the robbery.

being collected on another day, and the haul was £3000 on this occasion. It was one of two similar payroll snatches made on the same day, 13th July 1961.

Back at the factory the following day, with all of the benefit of hindsight, the cynics were full of talk about the company's ineffective arrangements, and the claim that our outriders were disabled by colliding with the back of our own van before they were attacked. I don't recall seeing any damage on the van to indicate that this was true, but whatever the circumstances, it must have been a frightening experience for the employees involved.

14 The Race Shop

At last, having acquired the most basic of skills and some modicum of academic ability, I was rewarded by a long spell in the Racing Department as an alternative to the production assembly line; and it did not disappoint. As previously described, separated from the main factory by the width of Burrage Grove, this holy of holies was a long, single storey building with its narrow end facing the road. At the back end was an office for the boss, Jack Williams, a small secluded office with a workbench behind it, and above these, in the loft space, was where the race shop spares were stored. Outside and behind the building was the access to the two separate underground caverns that housed the Heenan and Froude water-wheel dynamometers.

Standing at the door to Jack's office and facing towards the road, the main shop was laid out with engine assembly benches to the left and a lathe, cam profiling machine and small machine tools down the right-hand wall. Fixed-height bike assembly benches were arranged at an angle but parallel to each other down the centre of the building. At the far end, two bike building benches were laid parallel to the main building. These were defined as the 'Competition Department,' and work at that end, together with the dedicated personnel who worked there, was separately managed by Wally Wyatt. This was where special competition bikes were prepared, and where Vic Eastwood worked with Wally personally in the building of scrambles machines to his specific requirements. They had their own entry door at the top of a short flight of steps at the front of the building and, although under one roof, there was a very clear distinction between the two departments.

Apart from the excellent products and the care with which they were assembled, it was the people that really made the Race Shop interesting. At the top, of course, there was Jack Williams. Kind and friendly, even to the most junior apprentice, he cut an image of the classic absent-minded professor, dressed in tweedy sports jacket and with a pipe either in the corner of his mouth or in his outside top pocket. As seems to be the rule with these things, the pipe seemed to spend more time being re-lit than being smoked. He was keen to motivate me to pursue my studies and gain membership of the Institute of Mechanical Engineers, but at the time this seemed a far off and most unlikely possibility.

He loaned me a copy of his thesis on engine breathing and gas-flow that had recently been the vehicle for his own acceptance as a member, this being an alternative to academic qualifications as a route to membership. I was deeply interested in learning everything that I could from this respected man. Lying around in his office were perspex models of cylinders and cylinder head porting by which means and assisted by coloured smoke, he had studied the behaviour and mixing of gasses within the combustion chamber. Had computer modelling been available, it might have saved him a great deal of work.

His son, who would in later years become a star motorcycle racer himself, was not allowed in the Race Shop, and I think that his father actively discouraged his interest in racing. If true, that must have been a forlorn hope for a father who had been a successful racer himself. Peter did, however, visit occasionally. He knew most of the race mechanics and was privately racing a Velocette KTT. When the engine of this needed serious attention, such as a new big-end, Peter would appear at the back door that led into the private little workshop behind his father's office. There, an enthusiastic mechanic would discreetly solve his problem. I never knew whether Jack truly didn't see him, or whether he preferred to just turn a blind eye to the proceedings. I think that the latter was the more likely scenario.

Below Jack was Jim Boughen, in brown smock overalls and holding the authority of a chargehand. The atmosphere was always very competitive in the Race Shop, particularly between the engine builders. Each customer seemed to have a favourite person that he wanted to build his engine, believing sincerely

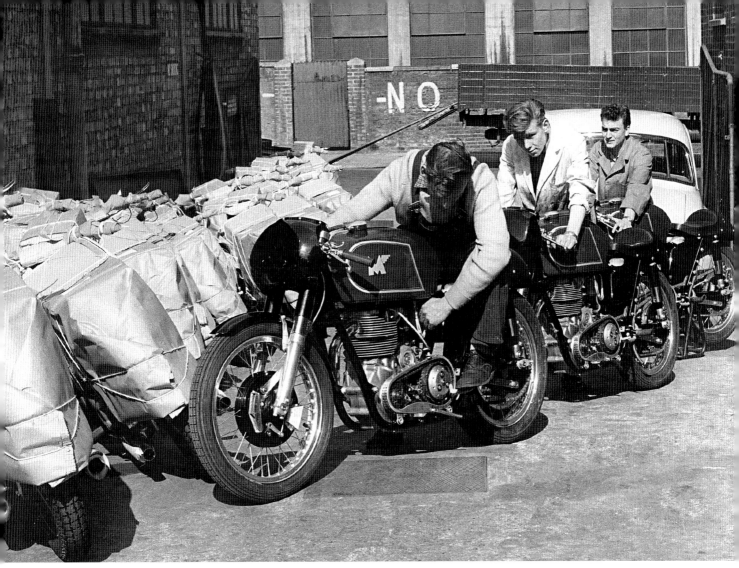

A trio of G50s is prepared for road test outside the Race Shop, while a batch of Matchless twins awaits dispatch. The works flat bed truck waits for the twins to be loaded. L to R: Jack Emmott, Derek Dixon and Tommy Mortimer
(Courtesy Mortons)

that particular engineer could gain a fraction of a brake horse power more than another. Jim was at the top of that pile, and was naturally the person to whom I reported. Some of the other engine builders couldn't help but show their jealousy of his position and his slightly closer relationship with Jack Williams. It was said that Jack always preferred Jim to accompany him when he wanted to test a new engine variation for himself, but the word in the shop was that Jim cheated on the dynamometer. It was almost certainly unfounded gossip.

It's incredible to think that it was possible to run a full blooded racing engine on open exhaust pipe and full power in a built-up area of south-east London without disturbing the neighbours, but that was what happened. As the exhaust outlets were adjacent to the nearby railway cutting, however, some passengers may have occasionally been treated to some interesting sounds as they passed by! Although you knew

when an engine was on test, it was amazing how quiet those underground test cells were at ground level. Inside, however, they were intimidating, and it's doubtful that health and safety regulations would allow them to be built today.

Approached by a steep steel ladder, you arrived at a spot immediately facing the dynamometer. The engine under test was to your left with the water brake control wheel immediately in front of you. To the right of the brake was a large electric motor used for starting the engine, with a hand lever to operate a clutch to engage it. A steel mesh guard covered a splined coupling shaft to the engine to protect the operator from flying debris in case of a catastrophic failure of the connection. Facing was a board with instruments showing revolutions per minute and specific fuel consumption. Over to one side were a barometer and a large scale chart that were used to find a correction factor by which to adjust the brake horse power measured according

If the test beds were quiet above ground, they were hell below. With the noise of an engine on full power, the fans and brake, the heat and oil from the engine and the gale of forced wind, all enclosed in a small underground room with limited means of escape, it was not a place to stay for too long. One of the worst jobs that I was given was to act as the third person to make adjustments while an engine was under full power. The objective in this instance was to determine the optimum length of an open exhaust pipe to maximize power output. In preparation, I had to make up a range of exhaust pipe extensions in something like one inch increments with a sleeve brazed on so that they could be slid over the shortened exhaust pipe. Standing alongside the engine, in the full air blast from the fans, I had to fit these extensions as directed by the brake operator. After a few minutes the exhaust pipe would be glowing red at the cylinder head and every adjustment had to be made quickly using pliers only to hold and replace the various extensions. It was not pleasant, but I did get my turn to operate the brake controls eventually.

There were many well known names in the Race Shop at the time, not least being Jack Emmott and Tommy Mortimer, but the regular engine builders seemed to be the two 'Arthurs'; Arthur Childs and Arthur Keeler. They were totally different and very competitive with each other. Arthur Childs was a more introverted character, while Arthur Keeler was noisy, brash and crude. He liked a drink and his main party-piece was to demonstrate his unique ability to speak a complete sentence whilst simultaneously belching! They were both highly skilled and respected race engine builders, and every race engineer believed that they could build a better engine than anyone else. They seemed to guard their minuscule secrets very closely and while each and every one of them individually were very supportive and taught me much about the meticulous care that needs to be taken to build a reliable high performance engine, I always felt that their special secrets were available to no-one. Perhaps most of it was bluff.

I loved the work, the care and the clinical attention to detail, whether it was the precision of the exact point of a valve opening on the timing disc or the simple cleanliness of the operations. It was also a joy to dismantle an engine that had been run exclusively on Castrol 'R' and witness the extraordinarily clean condition compared with the dirty mess usually found in engines run on the mineral oils of the day. The finished engines, 7Rs (350cc

to atmospheric pressure. More sobering was the panel of red-buttoned emergency stop switches mounted on the wall, and thoughtfully positioned behind your shoulder blades, so that you would collapse onto them in the event of a disaster!

Large diameter fans covered with mesh grilles were set into the walls in front and behind the engine to provide the necessary cooling. An assistant would be in attendance to add weights to a balance arm that would be lifted by adjustment of the water flow by the operator. He, or a second assistant, might also be required to make adjustments to the engine while under power.

It was in the question of adding weights to the balance arm that Jim's honesty was questioned. Some of his detractors would say that he would keep a little hand pressure on the arm to simulate extra weight. This would increase the apparent power output and keep secure his position as Jack's favourite assistant. It is unlikely that sufficient consistency could be achieved by this means and I finally concluded that this was just another example of the rivalry and jealousy between the mechanics rearing its ugly head. Jim was always willing to help me in my learning and I was grateful.

AJS) and G50s (500cc Matchless) were a joy to behold with their dull electron crankcases and gold cam chain drive covers. Like all good motorcycle design, they looked fast even when sitting on the bench. A G50 engine would occasionally be fitted to a scrambles bike experimentally but none ever found their way into a road machine. That always seemed to me to be a pity. They would have made interesting rivals to Norton's 'Internationals,' and they would undoubtedly have been better at keeping the oil inside the engine where it belongs!

During my spell in the department, this team was completed by Jack Emmott, the relatively diminutive Tommy Mortimer (relative because Keeler was a big man and one to avoid a fight with), and the always smartly dressed Eric Goodfellow. Eric was the 'frame' man who generally assembled the cycle parts and actually fitted the engines and gearboxes into the frames. Eric stood apart from the intrigue and rivalry that seemed to exist between all of the others. Always a gentleman, and usually wearing a tie under his brown smock overall, he became a good friend, and was always ready to explain anything that you wanted to know. He obviously loved his job and it showed. Tommy also worked on the engines but at the time he seemed mostly to be occupied on the machine tools or prototype cam grinding. In reality, everyone 'mucked in' to do whatever was necessary when the need arose.

My abiding memory of the Race Shop, however, is a statement made to me by the very well spoken and educated Eric Goodfellow. I had completed my time assisting with the building of engines and had now become accustomed to the precision and meticulous care that was required of my work. Torque wrenches were naturally used to ensure that everything was tightened correctly.

The day then arrived when I was moved on to work with Eric, and I looked forward to the experience as he was a very amiable character. The first task in hand was to fit the engine to a new 7R and, having manhandled the engine into position together, Eric left me to insert all of the remaining engine bolts and tighten them. I was naturally concerned at the responsibility being entrusted to me and called out across the shop as he walked away "How tight should they be, Eric?" The reply was not what I expected: "Bill, in racing, there is only one tight and that is f***ing tight!" Up to that point I hadn't realized that torque figures were (somewhat illogically I thought) only used in the engine build and nowhere else. To this day, I smile to myself as I'm reminded of his response whenever I'm tightening a bolt that is critical.

They were jokers, all of them. The workers in the Race Shop were either respected or envied by the rest of the factory workers. Some saw them as the cream of the fitters and were proud of the company's involvement in racing. Others simply saw them as a bunch of lazy jokers who had the spare time to play games, while they had to sweat it out on piece-work in order to take home a sensible wage.

There was an element of truth in both, of course. The meticulous care needed in the building of a race bike was necessarily slow, but also, when the pressure was on before a race, and especially before the Isle of Man Tourist Trophy races and the Manx Grand Prix, they would work all the unsociable hours imaginable. They did, however, have 'perks,' and the riders were known to give treats to their supporting mechanics to ensure that they remained dedicated to the task. It was not unknown to occasionally see a famous rider slip into the Race Shop via the back door laden with a crate of beer, and these events no doubt added to the feeling among many that it was not just the road that separated the Race Shop from the rest of the factory. It was a bit like the gulf between factory workers and staff, and the perks in the Race Shop were never anything like the perks received by the Purchasing Department at Christmas!

Many, therefore, considered that a spell in the Race Shop was a waste of time for an apprentice, but I was there to be educated as well as to enjoy myself. My object was to learn assembly, yes, but properly, using only the best fitting techniques available. I never regretted it for one moment, and when I later worked with the most skilled employees in the Tool Room, I discovered that some of the best were ex-Race Shop personnel.

It was fun though, for apart from the glory of working with these beautiful machines, the people enjoyed themselves with a never-ending war of practical jokes. Tools were wired to hidden magnetos to provide surprise electric shocks, and buckets of water were carefully balanced over locker doors, which were sometimes welded shut. The swarf from machined electron (magnesium alloy) castings was kept and carefully stored in readiness for impromptu (and dangerous) firework displays. One of the simplest and best that I saw was an enamel tea-mug belonging to one of the engineers, screwed to the bench through its base with a fibre washer under the head of the screw to effect a seal before being filled with tea. It is extremely funny when someone expects to pick up something light only to find that it is infinitely heavy!

One strange part about racing was the continental 'circus' and its associated characters that I was privileged to meet. These were the true racers, rarely world championship contenders, but people who literally lived for their racing. The principle was simple. Unlike in the UK, race circuits on the continent paid start money in addition to any prize money to every rider who started a race. This could, therefore, provide a basic projected income (of not very much) to assist a carefully planned visit to as many continental race meetings as possible. What was needed then was a minimum of two bikes, say a 350 and a 500 (so that you could enter as many races as possible) and an old van in which to transport them. This vehicle would then double as sleeping accommodation for the rider. Providing that both the bikes and the van remained reliable and accidents were avoided, the rider might earn just enough to survive the summer and race another year. Of course, there was always the hope of a major win and big prize money or even fame to spur them on.

I have no doubt that they also did casual labour while on tour to supplement their meagre income, but in the winter they would be back at the factory. Initially they would camp in their vans in the back street behind the factory until the weather became too severe, whereupon they would seek cheap lodgings, sometimes with another colleague at the factory. With luck, the company would employ them through the winter, or they would find other

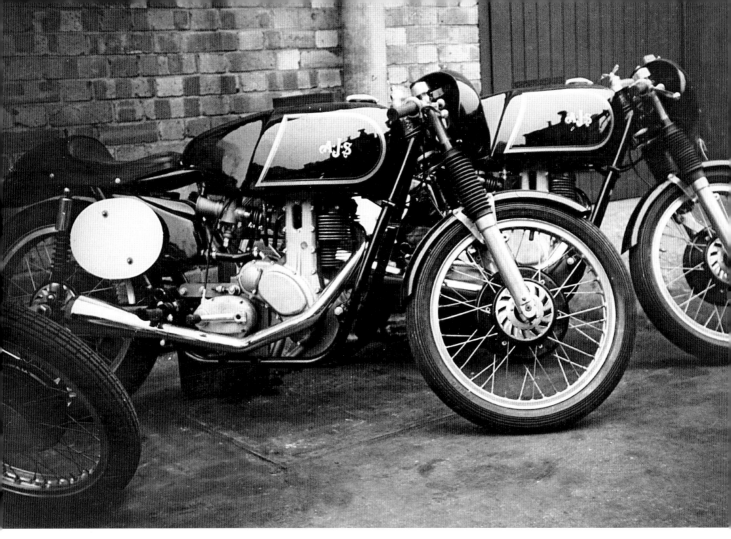

The last 7Rs to be built stand outside the race shop awaiting delivery.

local work in order to pay for the spares or servicing of their race bikes in preparation for the new season ahead. It was the life of a gypsy racer and, as an apprentice, I was fascinated by their alternative lifestyle. The reality of their financial position, however, was only too clear when they would bring in prizes gained from the past season, a silver cup or a watch perhaps, to trade for cash to finance their survival through the long winter. Some returned every year but, unfortunately, some never did. Such was the unpalatable cost of motor sport in the 1950s.

15 The Tool Room

The Tool Room (and in the peculiar structure that was AMC, together with the Tool Room Extension), was the department where all of the jigs, fixtures and press tools were made. These tools had a relatively long life, and enabled the operators to make precision components repeatedly, without the need for a high level of skill. The extension performed the same function as the main Tool Room, but additionally, was frequently involved in prototype manufacture and other interesting or unusual work.

As described previously, a new extension had been built in the early 1950s to house the new machine tools installed by the Alfred Herbert Machine Tool Company. On the top floor of this sat the Tool Room Extension and the Gearbox Assembly Shop. Behind the extension, and separating the main factory from the Plumstead Road entrance, was the new Design Drawing Office, which formed a second storey over the Accounts and Production Planning Departments. Only on the top floor of the new building was this section ever referred to as the 'extension,' because it was the only floor which was occupied by an extension of an existing department, all of the others being self contained and new. In the Tool Room, the new building was separated from the rest of the factory by very large, automatically-controlled fire doors, which were permanently open. Inside, therefore, there was no visible separation of the Tool Room, but the personnel on either side of that fire door considered themselves to be totally different from those on the other side, and in most ways they were. The staff that worked in the extension seemed to be that bit wilder, perhaps more creative, and definitely people who worked hard but hated to be 'managed.' Not all of them were particularly highly skilled, of course, but the joy was that they worked as a team and supported each other.

This was the 'Holy Grail' when it came to the concentration of skilled personnel, and where I was most fortunate to be placed in the latter years of the apprenticeship after the basic engineering skills had been acquired. They were a great bunch of people who

had (mostly) been selected either for their high precision on a specific type of machine, or for their ability to work creatively. A few appeared to have graduated there based on precision fitting skills that had been gained in the Race Shop.

They worked truly as a team and helped one another without showing that competitive rivalry that had existed in the Race Shop. The attitude was that there was no engineering problem they could not solve, and I cannot express sufficiently the gratitude I have for what these people taught me. The whole of my subsequent career was built on the foundation of the engineering knowledge and life skills that were learned in that department. The academic qualifications gained pale into insignificance when compared with that education.

It is not an illusion. Many times in subsequent employment, I've held positions of authority over more academically qualified and undoubtedly more intelligent people than myself, and have been able to manage the situations without difficulty. Their ability in their own specialized field was often greater than my own, and at first I was not confident and was surprised at what was happening. It took a little while for me to then fully appreciate the true value of the practical training that I had received and how it now enabled me to use these various specialist skills and apply them to practical use. That realization was accompanied by a much needed boost to my confidence. Looking back, I feel sorry for those less fortunate who missed out on a practical education of this level of quality. More than that, I feel even greater sorrow for our country in that such dedicated apprenticeships are no longer available to the current generation. Much is passed on from one generation to the next in the field of engineering, and we have lost a great deal in neglecting the valuable heritage that had been established since the industrial revolution.

In this department I learned how to drill holes with a simple drilling machine to a position tolerance of only a few thousandths of an inch, and to make just about anything. I was fortunate to

Tool Room Extension showing, L to R, my mentor Eddie Pettit (1), Wilf Graham (2), Charlie Sylvester (4) and Bill Mitchell (5).

be placed under the wing of Eddie (actually Edwin, but he never used that name, of course!) Pettit. Although they operated as a team to help one another, Eddie was the acknowledged leader and worked on the number one bench in the corner. He was supremely confident and there was little that he could not make, but he was modest in the extreme. He patiently taught me all that I could absorb and treated me like a son. My debt to that man with regard to my education is greater than any other.

Sadly, after AMC finally closed, Eddie secured employment managing a Government Centre that provided an occupation for disabled persons and those with learning difficulties. With his patience and wide ranging skills he was very popular, and soon introduced simple production techniques to improve the output. The staff was motivated by this, and profits rather than

losses soon became the order of the day. I remember that Eddie was totally destroyed when, eventually, the management summoned him to the office one day and told him to stop what he was doing. Making profit was risky as they might be in danger of losing their government grant! He eventually succumbed to a brain tumour before his time and the world lost a great man; an unsung hero.

They were a sociable crowd and were always arranging trips to see shows at theatres in London or organizing car rallies in the summer. They were a great deal of fun, but my only claim to fame was once winning the wooden spoon after getting hopelessly lost in the MG TC, and arriving at the finish from the wrong direction!

The Tool Room

Fellow apprentice Terry Wetherfield is presented with the honours by Wilf Graham of the Tool Room Extension, while apprentice Bernard Copleston stands behind.

Eddie Pettit takes the winner's prize, while Ted Tuff gets the wooden spoon. Bernard Copleston and my brother Bob look on in the car park at Bodiam Castle.

16 The eternal optimist

'Being an eternal optimist' is a criticism often levelled at me, along with that of 'day dreamer' but I make no apology. I believe that it's good to have dreams and ambitions, because they give you a goal in life, and keeping the dream alive helps you to focus on actually achieving it. T E Lawrence (of Arabia) was a devoted motorcyclist, and his words about motorcycling are worthy reading. He also had some words of wisdom about dreams that are worth repeating:

"All men dream, but not equally; those who dream by night in the dusty recesses of their minds, wake in the day to find that it was vanity; but the dreamers of the day are dangerous men, for they may act their dream with open eyes to make it possible. This I did."

The significance of having ambitious dreams did not dawn on me until later in life, long after my time with AMC, when I purchased my first cruising boat, a clinker-hulled 'Corribee' built on the banks of Loch Corrib in Ireland. This 21ft sloop was a thing of beauty, with its varnished mahogany planking, but it was not until the purchase had been completed that I remembered having visited the London Boat Show as a teenager and gazing longingly at that very same craft. I rushed home and searched through my old paperwork and found the very leaflet that I had kept from that boat show all those years before. Without realizing it, I had been subconsciously working towards that dream all the time! Similar experiences have been repeated since that date, and I still have my dreams! The subject matter here, however, is to relate the story of the day that my optimism and supposedly well founded logic, failed me disastrously.

My day-to-day transport had progressed as the apprenticeship developed and the pathetic remuneration crept upwards with painful slowness. The B33 had been traded in at Valentine Motors, Bromley, for a very immaculate 1957 Velocette MAC (TUC 574) which served me admirably for many years. This had been joined by the 1947 MG TC (LPE 647) which became my first successful venture into car ownership. Again, still lacking terribly in knowledge of motor cars or in the art of negotiation, it was purchased from a slightly more respectable-looking car dealership in Brownhill Road, Catford. Parked on the pavement, it looked lovely, with its black coachwork, and it had a hood! I was blind to everything else, including its oddly spoked spare wheel and dubious mechanical condition. With no car-owning friends to guide me and no-one in the family able to take it for a test drive, I gambled. I had rebuilt a motorcycle before. How difficult can it be to rebuild a car?

I was about to find out when I soon discovered just how tired the engine and gearbox were. Whilst I had managed to buy the car, I still could not afford to run it, so, while I saved for tax and insurance, I rebuilt the engine and gearbox on the dirt floor of the same Nissen hut garage that had housed my previous attempts at car ownership. To my amazement, with the minor exception of a tendency to jump out of third gear, the exercise was totally successful, and served to boost my confidence considerably. This MG meant a great deal to me and served me faithfully and reliably for several years.

It was the vehicle in which I taught myself to drive. I am ashamed to say that my practice was entirely illegal. To my mind it was a simple choice; I could either buy a car or pay for driving lessons, but not both. My first driving attempt was made in London under cover of dense evening smog which made me feel inconspicuous while I learned how to control the car. There were worrying moments, though. Once, I parked in a surprisingly empty London street, and when I returned to the car I was dismayed to find a uniformed policeman standing alongside it. The game was surely up? The policeman politely informed me that I should not be there as the road had been cleared of vehicles to enable a major parade to assemble there. He then proceeded to ask

My prized MG TC before the accident.

about the car. Apparently he had owned one once and wanted to talk about it. However, I was becoming anxious in case he should request to see my driving licence, and I just wanted to leave. Thankfully, he didn't ask.

On another occasion, while driving to work and still before I'd passed my test, I was approaching a policeman on point duty at a road junction, when the car jumped out of gear. I had forgotten my usual trick of holding it in with my left knee on the over-run! Unfortunately, I was wearing an ex-US air-force combat jacket which had draught-sealing straps at the wrists. It was winter, and the hood was up with side-screens in place. I had just given a clear hand-signal through the tiny flap in the side-screen of my intention to turn right, when the wrist-band hooked on the external door lever. My left hand was essential for steering. I was, therefore, unable to re-engage a gear and, much to the PC's frustration, coasted slowly to a stop at his feet before I could disentangle myself. Fortunately, his priority was to keep the traffic moving rather than question me about my driving proficiency!

The driving test: When the date for my first test appointment came around, it had been snowing for a few days and the roads were very icy. I didn't consider this to be a serious problem so, having taken the day off work for the occasion, I duly turned up at the appointed time. I parked in the next street temporarily, before affixing the 'L' plates, and then drove around the corner hoping that no-one would see me arrive. To my disgust, the office was closed. A notice on the door informed me that all tests were cancelled due to the bad weather. Having ridden to work in all weathers for the past five years on two wheels, I found driving a car on ice positively easy by comparison, and was disappointed at the enforced delay while I waited for another appointment.

The first test had been scheduled to take place at Lee, but the waiting list was so long that, to gain an earlier appointment, I switched to Sidcup. It was further to travel but I wanted to be legal as soon as possible. The weather was still cold, but there was early sunshine and, with the hood down on the MG, I enjoyed the drive to the test station. The look on the examiner's face should have given me an indication that he was less than impressed with my choice of vehicle. Worse was to come, however, as the wintry sun disappeared and it started to snow! The hood was still down, of course. As the test proceeded, the poor examiner raised his collar and sank ever lower into his seat to avoid the

The view toward the access road, with the MG TC in the right-hand corner. The corner of my Father's garage can just be seen to the right.

worst of the blizzard. When the driving was over, I answered all of the *Highway Code* questions correctly, and then he gave me the piece of paper. He levered himself up out of the car and, with a hefty slam of the door, said nothing but "You've failed!" It was a bad day. To be fair, it wasn't my best driving performance, and I had obviously not been deliberate enough in letting him see that I was using my rear view mirror, which was the official reason eventually given for my failure.

By the time of the second appointment, again at Sidcup, I was desperate to pass and keen to do some serious motoring in the MG without the spectre of possible detection hanging over me. By now it was early springtime and the hood was permanently down. Again, my mood was good as I enjoyed the drive and this time the examiner smiled when he saw the car. When we had completed all of the tricky manouvering parts of the test, he directed me onto the local by-pass and invited me to increase the speed. He was obviously enjoying the sunshine and this open-air break from the daily tedium of small saloon cars and nervous drivers. At the end of the drive, I at last had that precious pink slip in my possession. There is no better feeling.

In retrospect, I'm horrified at the way that I learned to drive. At the time, however, there seemed to be little alternative. The fact that I didn't have a qualified driver alongside me (what could he do in an MG TC anyway?) and didn't have 'L' plates affixed, seemed trivial details to my inexperienced mind. I always carried 'L' plates in the car in case I ever found a qualified passenger wanting a lift! I was insured after all, but no-one had advised me of my insurance company's probable attitude should I have had an accident. Happily, this was never put to the test. As far as I was concerned, I had paid my premium, ergo I was insured! It is probably true to say that if I'd had a full understanding of the facts at the time, I would never have learned to drive a car until much later in my life. There followed many enjoyable drives in that car and there could not have been a more proud driver on the road. One day, however, that dream literally came to a crashing end.

An explanation of the scene is required. Our house was in Bawtree Road, one of four back streets located between New Cross and New Cross Gate stations that formed a rough square. Their 'gardens' (actually small concrete yards) were short relative

My jolly maternal Grandfather, Alf Parsons, in more familiar surroundings!

what passed as garages made from a motley assortment of corrugated iron sheeting and old house doors. Some were more easily recognized as old Nissen huts by their rounded roofs. The plot was owned by 'Blakey,' the local shoe-repairer in Woodpecker Road (was that his real name, I wonder?). He also drove the only remotely modern vehicle to be housed there; a grey, high roof Bedford 'Dormobile.' The rest of the shacks housed a variety of mostly pre-war vehicles, half of which never moved. For us local kids, it was a junkyard playground and a haven of hidden treasure, which for me, was quite literally just over the back wall. I rented a round-topped Nissen hut about halfway up the right-hand leg of the triangle and Dad rented the first one at the bottom of the left-hand leg, adjacent to the exit driveway and only a few yards (metres) from our back yard.

Having described the scene, the players numbered only two. There was me, a lanky 6ft 1in tall, just out of my teens, and my maternal Grandfather, Alf Parsons, who lived in the downstairs flat below us. Now, Grandfather Parsons was not built like me. He was short and rotund. A round, jolly person, he would have a go at anything in spite of his now being too close to 80 for comfort. He was a lovely character and a qualified driver of steam trains. He loved his trains and was well respected by his colleagues. It was convenient for him that he retired just as his beloved steam engines were heading for the scrap heap.

It was a lovely sunny day during the week and, for me, a rare day off work. The MG had been rebuilt and was still 'tight' following the recently completed engine rebuild. New bearings, piston rings and seals had been fitted and I was keen to put some miles on the clock and enjoy a day's freedom in the open air. The car was clean and I was ready to go. We had some trouble after the rebuild that had necessitated a tow initially to get the car started, so tight was the new engine. This day proved no exception and the battery soon tired of the effort. Swinging on the handle, easy before the rebuild, now seemed impossible and, try as I might, I could not swing the engine over fast enough to make it start. Help was needed.

It's amazing just how quiet and deserted the busy back streets of South London can be in the middle of the week. There was not a soul around. Everyone, including my Mother and Father, was at work, and my younger brother was at school. My Grandmother had passed away some years earlier. I needed a push but the only person around was my ever helpful Grandfather. Clearly his age precluded such strenuous effort from being considered. At that fateful moment, the master plan came into my mind and its logic seemed infallible.

I had been the first person in our family to own and drive a motor car. Grandfather Parsons had never sat behind the wheel of a car before, but he could drive just about any steam train. Surely that must have been a much more demanding and complicated business than driving a car? There was a gentle slope down from the apex of the triangular yard to the exit driveway. I reasoned that I could push the car to the top of this slope. This done, I sat Grandfather behind the wheel. Even using all of the seat adjustment, he could barely see over the bonnet or reach the pedals. However, with the aid of cushions borrowed from the house, some semblance of a normal driving position

to the number of houses in each street, and this left an enclosed space that the 'gardens' backed onto. Because one of the roads was very short, this space was actually approximately the shape of an equilateral triangle with No.13's back yard sitting roughly in the middle of the base. There was a gap between the back of the houses in Bawtree Road and the side of the first house in the adjacent Ludwick Road. This provided a narrow access track from the enclosure which led from the bottom left corner of the triangle to the road. Wooden gates at the entrance provided nominal security, and a short two-rung ladder chained to our back wall provided our own private entrance.

The area had apparently once been a builder's yard, but after the war when I knew it, it was a dirt yard surrounded by was achieved, and the old chap, game as ever, seemed to be enjoying the prospect of his first drive.

What could be simpler? With the hood down to enable me to get to the controls quickly and the tick-over adjustment set abnormally high, I engaged second gear and turned on the ignition. The instructions to Grandfather were simple: 'Push the big left-hand (clutch) pedal to the floor.' I start pushing. When I say 'Now,' take your foot off the left-hand pedal. The engine should fire. When I say 'Now' again, push both of the big pedals (clutch and brake) to the floor and hold them there. The theory was that this would happen in a very short distance and I would then run up behind the car, reach in, slip the gear lever into neutral and the job would be done, the engine running sweetly on the fast tick-over. Easy isn't it? No steering or driving skills required! Unfortunately, in this life, theory is not always translated into practice.

I started pushing. "Now!" Grandfather released the clutch pedal as instructed and the engine fired immediately as expected. The car accelerated smartly, throwing a shower of stones at me as the rear tyres bit into the dirt. "Now!" I shouted again and Grandfather dutifully tried to obey. Unfortunately, the sudden acceleration had unseated and disoriented him and the only pedal that he managed to find was the throttle! This he pressed hard and there was no way that I could catch him. The concrete wall of our back yard and the narrow exit drive were approaching fast. Could he steer it down the exit road and buy enough time to find the brake? The answer came soon enough as he made a valiant attempt to steer for the exit and avoid the solid wall. The car hit the left hand corner of the last garage on the right which, of course, was the one that my Father rented. The offside front wheel went through the door while the rest of the car stayed outside. The left hand door post was neatly wedged against the offside front brake-plate between the radiator and the front wing, when the plot finally came to rest.

Typically, Grandfather took the whole experience in his stride. Once I had established that he hadn't hurt himself, he tried to console me with his confident assertion that "we'll soon straighten this lot out." It wasn't so easy when my parents arrived home from work. Dad took the repairs to his garage philosophically enough (the door post had been moved and the repaired doors never did hang properly again) but my Mother gave me a terrible dressing-down for my stupidity and for trying to kill her Father! She showed little sympathy for the plight of my precious MG. Oh for the wisdom of hindsight!

It was to be many weeks before the MG was mobile again. The offside front wheel was destroyed and the axle had been moved back, breaking the offside front spring. The lovely pointed shape of the front wing was now flat and pointing at the road, but thankfully, the door post had missed the radiator and headlamp. The only memorable and historically significant part of the repairs regarding AMC was sourcing a new pair of front springs from a gentleman in Folkestone. For this journey (in pouring rain) I borrowed a prototype 200cc 'G4' from the Experimental Department. If you have never heard of this bike, I wouldn't be surprised and you will have missed nothing. It was one of a pair of ill-fated prototypes (G4 200cc and G6 250cc) that were conventional overhead valve singles with square-finned barrels. They were intended to replace the Matchless G2 and G5 models but never made it to production and I doubt that they survived. This particular example was truly awful, and I clearly remember my dismay when on the homeward journey with the TC springs lashed across the pillion seat, it struggled to climb the hills. The journey on this pathetic machine seemed to take forever. I came home with the springs as a trophy and another serious bout of bronchitis. Was I older and wiser? No, that would take a little longer.

17 The Drawing Office

To work in the Design Drawing Office had always been my main ambition as I worked my way through the machine shops and other experiences. Much as I had loved the fun and time spent in the Race Shop, and had gained such confidence from what I had learned in the Tool Room, these were only stepping stones to give me the basic knowledge to be able to design.

I was not to be disappointed. At the time of my transfer, the Drawing Office was being managed by Horace Watson. A kindly and gentle person, he was in the latter stages of his career, and it was clear that a graduate engineer, Tony Denniss, was being groomed to take over from him. Tony was a slightly eccentric character but gained my immediate respect by his acknowledgement that he did not possess the vital practical experience to enable him to manage the department effectively. Before accepting the full time responsibility, therefore, he opted to go through a form of compressed apprenticeship and worked the first part of each day in the factory. It was strange to see this normally immaculately suited character return to the office in a boiler suit dripping in cutting oil. He still wore a collar and tie under his overalls though!

Tony was a bit of a mystery character, and his private life and relationships were always a big secret with him. Eccentric? He had three passions: a 750cc Royal Enfield twin, Jaguar saloons (not always in the best of condition) and Scalextric. These preoccupations provided the office with plenty of amusement. Now, Tony was the archetypal English gentleman, and his Jaguar would always be seen complete with bowler hat and rolled umbrella on the rear parcel shelf. However, he had an aversion to paying for his road fund licence, and none of his vehicles were ever taxed in spite of the senior management position that he held. It was simply a matter of principle with him. The Government did not spend all of the money on improving the roads and, therefore, no reason to pay for a 'road fund' existed.

Tony's route home took him close to where I lived and, on one occasion when I had just returned one of the company's test bikes, he offered me a lift in his Jaguar, a rare luxury for me. As we approached the junction at the top of Deptford High Street, the traffic lights turned against us, and to my horror, a policeman was standing in a shop doorway close by the car. I saw his eyes survey the car and his move towards us as he spotted the vacant space on the windscreen where the tax disc should have been.

Tony stared straight ahead and doing his best to speak without opening his mouth, whispered "Lock your door and don't look at him." I obeyed. The policeman came to my door, knocked on the widow and indicated that he wanted Tony to open it. Tony looked back, shrugged his shoulders and held up both hands in a gesture of incomprehension. The performance was repeated several times. By now I was quite petrified at what would happen next, but Tony remained cool as the process was repeated. Eventually, the lights changed to green and, this being the height of the rush hour, horns started blaring around us as the junction headed for gridlock. Frustrated by the situation, the policeman relented and with a rapid gesture waved us on. I sat there in disbelief that this refined and educated professional could act in this way. Such was his eccentricity.

Tony was one of the leading lights in the office. Being engineers, it was a matter of principle that nothing that could be purchased would ever be as good as that which was made, and the search for more power and grip in the model cars really did get out of hand. Some of the modifications were inventive, however, and they included a Mini with front-wheel drive and working steering (Ned Hooker's creation). Unfortunately, my apprentice pay prevented me from taking a serious part in these activities except as a 'guest' driver in a borrowed car. Older ex-apprentices Ned Hooker and Terry Wetherfield were the acknowledged champions, as I recall. In retrospect, I shudder to think of the real cost of these developments to our employer.

Motorcycle Apprentice

The staff in the Drawing Office was a motley crew of about ten draughtsmen, a tracer, and a technical clerk. The most senior was Eric Crouch, who rode an old Norton sidecar outfit. He was the one to go to if you had a mathematical problem. Alan Deakin was an amateur racer who dreamt of greater things. He kept a Guzzi single cylinder engine under his table at work and had injured his knee in a racing accident at Brands Hatch on a Ducati single, leaving him with a limp. He never seemed particularly dedicated to design work. I believe that he achieved a significant position with Ford later in life so perhaps he was right. Well known racer Frank Perris often joined the team in the winter months. Alan Sheath was envied as he did nothing else but work for the Racing Department and enjoyed regular discussions with Jack Williams. He went on to set up a very successful chain of greengrocery stores when he left. Another draughtsman was an ex-policeman who took forever to draw a half-scale side elevation of a G80CS scrambler. It was drawn on cartridge paper with every minute detail shown and was apparently wanted for a proposed catalogue illustration. He seemed to do nothing else all the time I was there, and I understand that when he left, he rolled the drawing up and took it with him! The subject was never mentioned again. Charlie Matthews was quite literally the cornerstone of the office, and sat in the corner opposite the tracer. His title was officially 'Drawing Office Clerk.' A knowledgeable man, he had come up through various departments and had obviously enjoyed a close relationship with the racing fraternity in the past. He had an encyclopaedic knowledge of part numbers, and took great care to protect and maintain the quality of the drawing records which, I must say, were superb. He had a wicked and cutting sense of humour but would never fail to be helpful. He was the rock on which the AMC drawing records were founded.

Ray Warren, another quiet and clever man, did nothing but gearboxes, and was the office expert on tolerancing. Indeed, few people realize that tolerancing is an art form in itself and its analysis is often treated as a quite separate exercise from design. Gearboxes, with the large number of moving components in such a small space are, therefore, a critical area of a motorcycle where tolerance build-up matters most. Tolerance analysis is an essential factor for any mass-produced component and cannot be dispensed with if selective assembly is to be avoided.

For reasons of economic manufacture, it's impossible to make a batch of components that are all exactly the same. Each component, therefore, has a maximum and a minimum size between which limits it is deemed to be acceptable. Tolerance analysis involves the theoretical assembly of all of the components, first assuming that they are all on maximum size limit and then again assuming that they are all on minimum size. If the assembly still works in both situations, then the tolerancing is acceptable. If not, tighter tolerance dimensions, involving more cost, selective assembly, or the use of shims may be needed to effect a solution. Nowadays it has become a forgotten subject that we take for granted. However, when we buy that spare part for a vehicle over the counter, tolerancing is the reason that it usually fits!

Ned Hooker was another apprentice and a character who graduated in one giant step from riding a tuned 50cc NSU 'Quickly' moped to a full blown and brand new Matchless 650cc G12 CSR. From his privileged position as an employee, he was able to oversee the build of his new machine from start to finish. On completion, it was a beauty. Ned was short in stature and he had specified it to be fitted with a very small trials pattern tank. This served to enhance the size of the engine and it was by far the best looking CSR that I have ever seen. Ned was also famous for a disastrous incident when he 'borrowed' a works sidecar outfit to see if he liked three wheels as much as two. It was unusual for the works to have a sidecar outfit around, but this one had been built for loan to a film company, presumably to gain some free publicity. Ned took the outfit out on his own up to Plumstead Common but on his return and taking the downhill left turn (negative camber) into the road behind the factory, the sidecar wheel came off the ground and Ned did the only thing possible and applied opposite (right) lock to bring it down. Unfortunately for Ned, one of the senior manager's cars was in the way! In typical fashion, youthful enthusiasm for motorcycles was accepted by the management and nothing serious by way of punishment ensued.

Like the rest of us, Ned was keen and rode his bike to work every day, rain or shine, summer and winter. It is hard to believe that we did this now, 'footing' on ice and snow like trials riders in London traffic! Before the winter came, we would coat all the chrome and other corrodible surfaces with a tacky substance that the company used on machines packed for export. It gathered dirt and the bikes looked awful but, come the spring, a quick hose down after a good painting with 'Gunk' de-greaser had the machines looking (and smelling!) as good as new again.

Smog was a serious and more insidious hazard that claimed many lives. It was the name given to the dense fogs that London used to suffer from, before the introduction of the Clean Air Act. As the name implies, the smog was caused by the smoke laden atmosphere, and the thickness of the smog is hard to describe to someone who has never experienced it. Apart from being seriously injurious to health, it is far thicker than any natural fog that I have ever known, and it literally brought London to a standstill on occasions. Like winter ice, it was just another ride to work challenge for us, and for once, motorcyclists were in demand. When the smog was at its worst, visibility was literally reduced to a metre or two and drivers of buses and similar vehicles with high mounted cabs found it impossible to see the road. The motorcyclist, with no windscreen to impair his vision, and feet with which he could feel the edge of the road, had a distinct advantage. On several occasions, a bus driver has asked me to lead him across a junction in these conditions. The authorities tried to help by lighting flares placed in the centre of the road, but their smoky flames seemed to add yet more to the chaos. For me at least, with a scarf wrapped around my face as a filter, the journey to work was achievable, but some, with longer distances to travel, found it impossible. On a few very bad days some of the Drawing Office staff, who had longer journeys to do, slept on the floor of the office as there was no other option.

These were the working colleagues and our way of life, but what of the bosses? I have mentioned Horace Watson. He was the outgoing Drawing Office Manager, an ex-Triumph man who

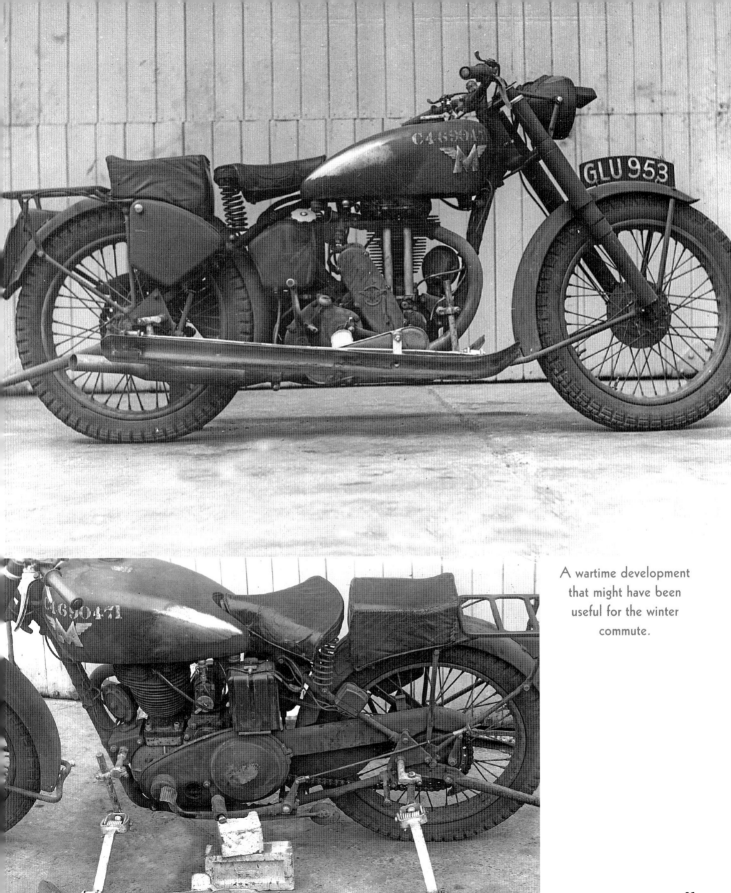

A wartime development
that might have been
useful for the winter
commute.

was promoted to work in the secluded office under the stairs leading to the drawing office. This was where development design was undertaken, and had been formerly occupied by another quiet and kindly gentleman, Phil Walker. Walker had visited the main Drawing Office occasionally and spent most of his time either speaking to Alan, the Race Shop draughtsman or to Horace Watson. By the books in his bookcase, he was obviously from the aircraft industry previously, and I only knew him by reputation as the designer of the 'G2/G5' motorcycles and creator of their unusual circular gearboxes. To my everlasting shame, it was not until some time later that I discovered that he was the designer of the original overhead camshaft R7/R10 AJS that formed the origins of the famous 7R 'Boy-Racer' after the war. I assume from his period of employment that he may also have played a significant part in the 'Porcupine' racer project. This would have explained his close association with the racing and development personnel, and I now wish that I had asked him more questions about his past. As I have said, however, he was a very senior and remote person and was unlikely to spend much of his time talking to an insignificant junior apprentice like myself. I cannot recall his leaving and assume that he retired quietly, as was his way.

The Drawing Office was always a fun place to work and did not enjoy a good reputation for industry. Necessary thinking time is always seen as idleness to those who have never tried to create something given only a clean sheet of paper and a pencil! Apart from Scalextric, the office held a weekly swimming session at Plumstead baths during (a probably extended) lunch-break. The journey was made possible by Geoff Josey, a young draughtsman who had joined us from Rolls-Royce and who became my best friend. Geoff was keen on trials riding, and owned a Greeves trials bike, but his regular transport was a Morris Minor van. This provided ideal, if crowded, transport for the large contingent from the Drawing Office which included our leader, all of whom had suddenly decided to keep fit.

One thing that I have never been good at is getting out of bed in the morning, and this failing manifested itself at its peak when I joined the Drawing Office, and often landed me into hot water with my new boss, Tony Denniss. Eventually, the repeated reprimands became tiresome and I rather foolishly decided to liven things up a bit. The Drawing Office was on the first floor. It was accessed from stairs at each end, one flight leading from the office entrance on Plumstead Road and the other being a stone staircase connecting to the factory. From the Plumstead Road entrance, there was a small lift to the office (the normal entrance) whose doors opened directly in front of the Manager's Office. Tony had the habit of anticipating my late arrival and would stand with his hands behind his back, like an old-time policeman, waiting to face me as the automatic doors opened. On this occasion, however, I stripped off my motorcycle clothes and placed my boots, neatly folded trousers and over jacket, topped by my gloves and helmet, on the floor of the lift and pressed the button to send it on its way. I then sprinted along the lower corridor and up the stone staircase to the far end of the office. I managed to get quietly seated at my drawing board without being seen before Tony emerged from his office to greet

I try Geoff Josey's Greeves trials bike but conclude that two-strokes are not my scene.

the empty lift! It caused a good laugh and to Tony's credit, he bore no lasting grudge. In fact, the episode only served to make me more aware of the stupidity of my irresponsible attitude to timekeeping, and I changed my ways forevermore thereafter.

On the serious side, I learned much in that office and have been eternally grateful ever since. As I may have mentioned, I could never get excited about the company's run-of-the-mill products which, in spite of the build quality, always seemed to be the 'grey porridge' of the industry. All of this changed during my time in the Drawing Office after the Group had purchased Norton. At last I became enthusiastic when, with the closure of Bracebridge Street in 1963, Norton production was moved into the plant at Plumstead. A gleaming new Dominator twin with chrome mudguards was parked in the central gangway of the

The new Norton is presented at the local cinema. Behind the bike are Bill Corm, Frank Pollard, George Batley and Alan Jones. Fred Neill and Bill Martin stand to the right.

office to speed our education, and these stylish machines slowly began to roll along our production line.

A reality regarding build quality needed to be faced, however. In the Drawing Office, we were at the sharp end of having to resolve engineering faults with the new products, some of which were a shock to us all. I may have privately regarded the AJS and Matchless road machines as 'grey porridge' but they were made with precision and quality, and the Plumstead Tool Room engineers were second to none.

One early incident was cylinder bore wear on the 'Jubilee/ Navigator' range. Products were being returned after very low mileages with worn out cylinder bores. Much to our surprise, the bores were found to be wearing sideways rather than front and back as is normal. Eventually it was found that the jig supplied

from Norton had been machined out of square. This error (an unheard of occurrence at Plumstead as such an item would have been scrapped immediately) had been known to the operator in Birmingham who had always set up the jig by packing under one side with cigarette packets before he started machining! A new jig was commissioned.

A more personal involvement came when I was charged with a project to investigate the incidence of a foul that was occurring between the front mudguard and the frame on the 'Featherbed' framed models, causing a recurrence of dented front mudguards.

Having carefully drawn all of the component parts, assembled to scale, with the front springs fully compressed, in theory there still remained adequate clearance between the

Motorcycle Apprentice

frame and the mudguard. Even allowing for wear and deflection of the forks and a loose steering head bearing, there was no way that a foul should have been possible. Having double-checked every dimension of my drawing, the only thing left to do was to check all of the components involved to ascertain that they were made to the drawings specification. You can imagine my surprise when I discovered that it was the famous 'Featherbed' frame itself that was in error and had always been made so! From memory, the headstock tube was welded at 24 rather than the intended 26 degrees from the vertical as specified on the drawing. It served to illustrate a classic engineering mistake when measuring a dimension that is just to one side of a major graduation on a rule or protractor (in this case 25 degrees) when it is so easy to read to the wrong side of the mark. The solution was the introduction of long 'Roadholder' forks though I doubt that the reason why is well known. I have always been a great fan of this frame's handling qualities but after this experience I often mused about whether this famous frame would have handled as well had it been made to the drawing? Or, perhaps more likely, was it just a draughtsman's error when he made the drawing retrospectively from a prototype frame? Much, much later in life, around the time of the 1989 reunion meeting held in Beresford Square, we were riding our 1957 wide-line 'Featherbed' International Norton and were forced to make a straight-line emergency stop. There was a bang and, on closer inspection, there was the old familiar dent in the front mudguard. The past had returned to haunt me once more!

In spite of all the problems, I still retained a great respect for the Norton factory and its products. It was just another way of working, and I believe that the Vincent company operated in much the same manner. It was not the AMC way, but Norton had been effective for a long time, and still produced better-looking motorcycles, in my humble opinion. Our own products were not without their problems, of course. The new petrol tank design, with its centrally-welded spine, was a constant source of failure until a mounting method was found to insulate it from the vibration on the twins. We also suffered stylistically when those dreadful cast tank badges were introduced. The old formula was well engineered. 'Dressing it up' added nothing to the product and, sadly if anything, degraded it.

18 Indentures & real work

The five-year wait to be able to earn sensible money passed relatively quickly. Time always passes this way when you're busy. The apprenticeship plus day release at college, together with evening classes to gain endorsement qualifications meant that I was busy. When that was added to the active social life of a teenager and evenings chasing girls, every moment of each week was filled to the point of exhaustion.

Eventually the big day came for the presentation of the indentures. How proud I was to receive indentures from one of the country's major motorcycle manufacturers! When my friend and fellow draughtsman, Geoff Josey, had joined the company, I distinctly remember Tony Denniss, the Drawing Office Manager, excitedly coming out into the office to report how impressed he had been to see Geoff's indentures from Rolls-Royce in Derby. He vividly described their presentation in a leather wallet inscribed on the front with the classic 'RR' insignia. It seemed to me to be entirely appropriate considering the five years of hard work on derisory wages that it had taken to earn them.

There was no such luxury at AMC. Mine came in a plain brown envelope but they are no less a treasured possession for that. They were presented at the Annual Apprentice Prize Giving Ceremony, and with them came the most welcome offer of a permanent position as a draughtsman in the Design Drawing Office. An ambition had been achieved.

Soon after the ceremony, my old mentors in the Tool Room asked to see what indentures were like and I proudly took the very legal-looking document to show them. The document listed all of the departmental training that I had experienced and concluded with a qualification of 'Design Draughtsman.' To my surprise, this caused disgust and consternation amongst my peers and I was shocked by their reaction. I had seriously underestimated

Indentures.

AGREEMENT OF APPRENTICESHIP

This Agreement made the ___30th___ day of ___December___ One thousand nine hundred and ___Fifty eight___ between ___William Alfred Cakebread___ (hereinafter called "the Apprentice") a minor of ___Sixteen___ years of age on the ___9th___ day of ___November___ One thousand nine hundred and ___Fifty seven___ of ___13, Bawtree Road, New Cross, London, S.E.14___ and ___William Henry Cakebread,___ (hereinafter called "the Guardian") of ___13, Bawtree Road, New Cross, London, S.E.14___ and ___Associated Motor Cycles Ltd.,___ (hereinafter called "the Employer") of ___44, Plumstead Road, London, S.E.18.___

WITNESSETH that with the consent of the Guardian testified by the latter's execution of this Agreement the Apprentice has agreed to serve the Employer, and the Employer has agreed to accept and pay for such service upon the conditions hereinafter contained.

1. The Apprentice and the Guardian severally agree with the Employer as follows :—
    (1) The Apprentice will as from the ___1st___ day of ___September___ One thousand nine hundred and ___Fifty eight___ serve the Employer for a total period of ___Five___ years of service, each year to consist of fifty-two working weeks calculated in accordance with the provisions of this Agreement, which total period is hereinafter called "the period of service."
    (2) The Apprentice will during the period of service—
        (a) observe and be subject to the conditions of employment contained in the schedule annexed hereto ;
        (b) obey the lawful orders of the Employer or his representatives ;
        (c) promote to the best of his ability the interests of the Employer.
    (3) The Apprentice will not during the period of service—
        (a) reveal the secrets of the Employer's business ;
        (b) do or suffer to be done any damage or other injury to the property of the Employer or his customers ;
        (c) absent himself, except in the event of sickness, from the service of the Employer without his permission or consent ;
        (d) take part in any labour dispute which may arise between the Employer and any of his employees or in which the Employer and any of his employees may be involved, nor during the continuance thereof refuse to do any work which the Employer may lawfully require him to perform.

2. In consideration of the said obligations undertaken by the Apprentice and the Guardian, the Employer agrees with the Apprentice and the Guardian that, subject to the provisions of this Agreement, he will for and during the period of service—
    (1) receive the Apprentice into his service and, subject to the fulfilment by the Apprentice of the said obligations, allow the Apprentice to continue therein until the expiration of the period of service ;
    (2) observe the conditions of employment and pay to the Apprentice in respect of his service wages at the rates contained in the schedule annexed hereto ;

Happiness is an MG (with a strong luggage rack re-chromed courtesy of AMC, of course!).

their pride in the craftsmanship that they had passed on to me. "Design Draughtsman? Any bloody fool can push a pencil! You are a qualified toolmaker. That document is worthless! Take it back and get it amended!"

I thought about it for a while, considered future job interviews and the feelings of these people that I respected so much. Finally, I plucked up the courage to approach the Personnel Manager with my dilemma. On the one hand, I really didn't want to be labelled as just a toolmaker as that in isolation had connotations of manual work only. I dearly wanted recognition of the academic achievements that had also been made, and needed the document to be the basis for the start of a career in design. I need not have worried. The Personnel Manager was completely understanding of the situation and had only chosen to state the highest position that, from his perspective, I had achieved. It was but a simple matter to add 'Toolmaker' as an

additional qualification and everyone was happy again.

My only bitter disappointment had been my failure to become an Associate Member of the Institute of Mechanical Engineers. To achieve this, it was necessary to gain a Higher National Certificate in Engineering, plus several endorsements in other related subjects. In my case these included Marine Engineering and Metallurgy. Unfortunately, those that govern our education system changed the rules during my time at college and set a final date after which this means of entry into the Institute would be barred. There were simply not enough hours in the week to be able to study and pass all of the exams by the set deadline and, once again I became disenchanted with academic qualifications. It was also a bitter pill to swallow in that we had used Batchelor of Science degree papers as practice for our Higher National Certificate examinations and could do them with ease! As an apprentice, I was doing a five and a half day week, working 7.00am to 7.00pm most weekdays, and studying three evenings a week at college trying to achieve a qualification that some rich kid in college had all week to do. To cap it all, his BSc. degree carried a higher status than my HNC in the world of employment! It all seemed grossly unfair at the time.

There were occasions later on when it was suggested, based on patented designs and specific fields of experience that I had specialized in, that I should gain entry to the Institute by writing a paper on a specific subject. By that time, however, life had become very full with management responsibilities and I decided to forget about the pride of having letters after one's name and to concentrate instead on achievements that gave me more personal satisfaction.

During the latter part of my career, an expert personality profiler interviewed me and commented on his surprise that, irrespective of anything that had been achieved, I never needed anyone else to know about it! This was a throw-back perhaps, to that early rejection of the need for third party recognition. Only once did I have letters after my name. After filing several successful design patents, I joined the 'Institute of Patentees and Inventors.' That was fine until it was pointed out to me that the letters after my name:

W A Cakebread M.Inst.P.I. actually reads: W A Cakebread – Minced Pie! Needless to say, the title was never used!

Real work then began in earnest. With a junior draughtsman's salary replacing the apprentice's pittance, life became a little more comfortable and, for the first time in their lives, my poor parents received a small donation to the cost of my keep. The reward was small indeed. The Velocette had been sold after its Miller electrics corroded into dust, and the MG TC became my much loved daily transport. Happiness was a job that I adored and a drive to and from work every day that was relished rather than dreaded. The future looked bright. I was not rich but I felt like a king.

Life in the Drawing Office was interesting, with many opportunities to learn from others and to hone my design skills. Enthusiasm alone carried me on its wings. There were also benefits accorded to design personnel, such as being able to borrow test bikes, known as 'tea' bikes, to put additional mileage on them and (officially) for our education about the products that we were designing. This lessened the need to own one's own motorcycle and also helped to eke out the commuting cost of running the MG. My all-time favourite was 204 HLL. This was the Norton Atlas, black with a red tank, which *Motorcycling* magazine had used for a road test. The magazine headlined its report 'A Mountain of a Machine.' I loved to borrow it, and commuted on it as often as possible. The love affair ended at that same Deptford High Street junction where we had the incident in Tony Denniss' Jaguar. One cold and wet morning, while cranked over on the slippery surface, I was pitched off 'The Mountain.' The rear chain had broken and locked the rear wheel. There was no serious damage to either the bike or myself and I pushed it to my Father's workplace at Merryweathers in Greenwich High Road where I was able to raid his comprehensive toolbox and continue my (now slightly less confident) ride to work. Never a lover of vertical twins with

their attendant vibrations, I must admit that the raw power of this particular bike was a bit special.

On the subject of 'tea' bikes and road testing in general, it's amusing to reflect on how road safety fashions (I use the word advisedly) have changed since those days. It was at a time when 12 volt electrics were beginning to be adopted on motorcycles. The availability of magnetos had virtually ceased and the company was forced to follow the more economic fitment of coil ignition and alternators. The electrics (notably the alternator systems) were not as reliable as they should have been at that stage, and there was some bitterness in the company that the British motorcycle industry was being used as a test bed for the more lucrative car industry that the electrical manufacturers could not afford to upset.

At first, the use of 12 volt bulbs was a considerable problem as it was found that they would not survive the vibration periods experienced on our products. Various solutions for vibration-proof mounting of headlamps, etc. were experimented with and each had to be thoroughly road tested. This involved many thousands of miles of daylight testing with the lights on. With so many modern cars now wired so that they cannot be driven without the lights on and with motorcyclists being encouraged to 'be seen' by riding with their headlights on in daylight hours, I find it amusing that we were actually stopped by the police for this reason. We were threatened with prosecution because we were 'distracting other road users' by riding with our lights on! After several such incidents, we rode with the headlamp glass covered in black masking tape!

In a similar vein, there was a local band in Deptford that was harassed for the same reason when they painted their gig bus (an old single decker coach) in psychedelic colours. I guess that such incidents must be remembered in the context of an era where all police cars were black, ambulances were all white, fire engines were red, and their audible warning devices were all bells (of different tones, of course!).

As my apprenticeship terminated, I decided to become a responsible adult and change to a 'sensible' motor car. The decision was also somewhat forced upon me as I had by now left the parental home and had the responsibilities of rent and household bills to contend with. The decision to sell the MG was not an easy one and neither was the process of selling it. With no telephone, and only the *Exchange and Mart* as an affordable advertising medium, contact with potential buyers was not easy. In the end, it was purchased by a student from north of the Thames on the understanding that I would deliver the car and collect the payment. It was sold for much less than I had paid for it, despite the fact that it was now mechanically rebuilt and in much better condition than when I had purchased it.

I did not anticipate how emotional that delivery trip was going to be. I savoured every moment of that last drive across London, past my old school at Camberwell, over the river and up the Edgeware Road to the purchaser's address. The house was a large terraced one converted into flats and he lived on an upper floor. I collected the log book and my precious original workshop manual (lovingly bound in blue tracing linen for its protection from my greasy fingerprints) from the car and made my way up the

The TD2 parked outside the rented flat in Brockley. Such vehicles were all-weather transport in those days.

stairs to the door from where loud music was emanating. The room was quite full of students and a sea of faces greeted me. Some were playing guitars and the atmosphere was heady. The new owner seemed disinterested. He handed me the money and I gave him the log book and manual but he did not take them directly and simply said: "Put them over there." I offered the keys and to show him the car to complete the transaction but he said "Just leave it in the street," and didn't even bother to look at it. They carried on playing. I left with a heavy heart knowing that none of the care and attention that I had lavished on that car would be appreciated. It would surely be used and abused by someone to whom its value was insignificant. It was a betrayal on my part and the money in my pocket did not make me feel any better on the long underground train journey home.

Some of the money paid bills, and the rest eventually purchased a sensible side-valve Morris Minor. What a gutless contrast! Its breathless performance was suffered for a while,

but it wasn't long before another MG, this time a green TD2 (PYB 235) replaced it. This was best described as in 'average' condition but it was sound and reliable. Financially, however, it was a see-saw existence as I alternated between cheap motorcycles and sports cars as finances did or did not allow. That car again was sold at a loss and the purchaser never did pay me in full. I still had a great deal to learn about trusting people and trading with vehicles.

Eventually, I settled for the first of several MG Z series Magnettes (LJB 100) as a reasonable compromise between my beloved MG sports cars and sensible economic transport. Supremely comfortable and well appointed, these stylish saloons are under-rated, in my view. At the time, I used to refer to it as a 'poor man's Jaguar' and with another litre or litre-and-a-half under the bonnet it could have been a serious contender for that title perhaps.

19 Design – a career begins

Phil Walker, the quiet designer of the immortal 7R AJS, had worked in an obscure office hidden under the staircase that rose from the entrance to the Drawing Office at the Plumstead Road end of the factory. The office door looked almost like the entrance to a cupboard under the stairs. It was deliberately thus, both for security reasons and to ensure some peace and seclusion. Apart from anyone directly having business with the occupants, and a visit by the lovely girl who brought the tea twice a day, no-one ever had reason to go there. Horace Watson, former head of the Drawing Office, vacated the main office when Tony Denniss took over as manager. Phil Walker quietly disappeared (I assume that he retired) and Horace moved into his old office.

There he was joined by a new recruit in the form of Engineering Director, Charles Udall. At last, my opinion about Velocettes was vindicated as the company had just employed the man who was credited with the famous Mk VIII KTT racer, amongst many of his former company's other innovative products. It seemed strange to most of us that a man who had devoted almost the whole of his working life to loyally serving one company should suddenly join a competitor. We would not have been aware, however (as perhaps he had been), that the end of that company was fast approaching. Charles shared the same office as Horace Watson; Chief Engineer and Chief Designer, working together on the company's new products in the peace and solitude of their private office.

It should have made sense but they were opposites in character. It was Meriden against Hall Green, ex-Triumph against ex-Velocette, vertical twin against big single.

Horace was upright, warm and friendly, while Charles was dour and remote. There was no doubt that Udall held the senior position and frequented with the directors, while Horace accepted his lot as he worked towards his own retirement. Even their cars reflected their differences: Horace drove a dark blue Wolseley 1500 and parked it discreetly a street or two away from the factory. Charles, on the other hand, drove a gaudy and cumbersome red-over-white Vauxhall, with fins that would have looked more at home in America. The Vauxhall was always parked conspicuously outside the Service Department, and never seemed to fit with the man's sombre character.

My big opportunity came when I was invited to work with them in their private office under the stairs as their design draughtsman. It would obviously be a less sociable atmosphere than that which existed in the main Drawing Office, but I saw only the opportunity to learn from these experts in their field. On reflection, it is possible I was offered the position because no one else wanted to work with them in that atmosphere! It was certainly quite a contrast to the relaxed and congenial surroundings in the main office. I don't remember any noisy verbal exchanges between my bosses; they both conducted themselves like the gentlemen they were, but sometimes the tension ran high, and the atmosphere could be cut with a knife.

When I arrived, the stillborn 200/250cc G4 and G6 models had been drawn, and my task was to help speed up the completion of the new 800/850cc P10 overhead camshaft vertical twin, which at that time existed as a design scheme only. I sat at a drawing board in the corner facing the wall, the door to the office behind me. To my right, Udall sat at his desk looking toward the door. Behind me, Horace Watson sat at another drawing board facing Udall's desk. The arrangement was that Udall would direct proceedings while discussing design points with both of us. Horace did all of the leading design schemes at first, of course, while I (and later in the project, both of us), completed the detail drawings. As the project progressed, I did more of a combination of design schemes and detailing. It was a great experience for me as, in a relatively short period of time, Horace and I drew virtually every single component of that motorcycle. It was high pressure work with constant supervision, but I enjoyed it and learned much from both men.

Motorcycle Apprentice

A bonus in that office would be the company reps who visited regularly. Characters like Tyrell Smith, the Girling representative and former Rudge and Excelsior racer, had a long association with people like Watson. Their conversations were always interesting to listen to, and made a welcome break when Udall wasn't around.

An example of the education was cam design. There was no computer assistance at that time, so having decided on the formula for acceleration and deceleration rates for the valve, the cam centre of rotation was placed in the middle of the drawing board. The geometry of the valve actuating components was then rotated around it until a full 360 degrees of cam profile had been generated by the cam follower mechanism in each of its incremental positions. The drawing was then literally scaled in order to produce a large scale blank from which to cut the cams. This was typical of the projects that Udall would personally supervise over my shoulder, while Horace completed the frame drawing.

The engine was a rather odd one, and I was not particularly enthusiastic about it. Of unit construction, it had a five-speed gearbox, but the strangest feature was the timing chain that drove the double-overhead camshafts and everything else. It was very long, and led a tortuous path around the timing case before being led up plastic tubes (looking like Vincent push-rod tubes) to the camshafts and across the head. Many shook their heads and had visions of the chain cutting through the tubes, but Udall held firm, and the design worked; the close fit of the chain in the tubes preventing it from 'thrashing' out of control. Udall was innovative, and liked to try low-cost solutions to his designs. Sometimes they were clever, but occasionally their economy went a step too far.

Another of Udall's low cost design features on the P10 was the introduction of a spring blade type engine breather. Now, unlike a car engine where the pistons are at different points in the combustion cycle, on a large single or vertical twin engine, when the piston(s) descend, pressure builds up in the crankcase. The normal practice is to fit either a 'timed' valve or a spring-loaded one-way valve in the crankcase. By this means, the compressed air is allowed to escape on the down-stroke. The valve then closes on the up-stroke, forming a partial vacuum in the crankcase, a significant aid to keeping the engine oil-tight!

Udall's idea was to replace this valve with a simple reed valve fixed at one end and with its free end covering a large hole drilled in the crankcase. It was rather like the reed valve in a musical instrument and, unfortunately, it also behaved as one. I dutifully designed it, and on the test bed it seemed to perform adequately (on reflection, it

was probably omitted for performance tests on the test bed). When the first prototype was wheeled out for inspection by the directors, however, with a good coating of oil on the valve, the reed truly acted as a musical instrument. As the kick-starter was slowly depressed to prime the cylinders, the valve emitted the unmistakable low sound of flatulence! It was an embarrassing moment for all concerned. Some fine tuning was called for!

The best feature about this project was the pressure to get it finished. Immediately a part was drawn, it was made, and there was much liaison with my old colleagues in the Tool Room to get first the prototypes, and then the jigs and tools made. There was much scepticism, however, amongst the workers about the cost of the project, and I couldn't see any great leap of technical progress over the range of Norton twins. In my eyes, these were not only simpler, but were better looking to boot. The design staff as a whole did not have its heart behind the project, and dearly wanted to design a 'four' to compete with the Japanese. I believe that at one stage Tony Denniss actually approached the directors personally to express his concern that we should be developing something more advanced (a scheme for a four-cylinder machine already existed) but he was told that

The P10 engine on the test bed.

A surviving P10 at the National Motorcycle Museum. (Courtesy H McAllister)

they 'knew what the motorcyclist of today wanted.' If the story, as reported, was true, then they were so wrong.

We didn't know it then, but the scepticism of the shop floor workers was well founded. The Mini had been introduced, and the family sidecar outfit was thus made obsolete at a stroke. Big power motorcycling as a means of daily transport was on a slippery slope. The new machines coming in from Japan were technically advanced, oil tight and reliable. AMC was now spending another fortune tooling up for a third machine in a row that was out of date before it was finished, and was never to be launched. We had reason to be concerned. I loved the work, but at the same time I was wishing that we had more confidence in our future.

20 Racing cars – a new hope

Working more closely with members of the senior management perhaps provided a better insight to the lack of faith that existed throughout the company regarding the firm's direction. Manufacture of the racing bikes had finished; production output was falling. My Father had served the whole of his working life at Merryweathers and I had set my heart on a similar lifetime of working in the motorcycle industry, but it was clear that this was not going to be. It was time to move on.

Rather than watch the final death throes as this once proud manufacturer slid into oblivion, I decided that a change was necessary. The impossibly high cost of housing in the London area was another factor that was pressing a move elsewhere. For a brief period, it seemed that the solution would be found at a stroke when it was announced that AMC was planning to re-locate to new, modern, purpose-built premises at Sheerness on the Isle of Sheppey. It would not have been my first choice of somewhere to live, but it would be a considerable improvement on the back streets of New Cross. Housing was to be provided for any workers willing to move (many were not), and I was keen enough to view the proposed site one weekend. I wasn't aware of the politics or finances of the proposal at the time, but it came to nothing and I was back to square one.

Several of us, including my friend, Geoff, were feeling unsettled and concerned that there was no longer a long term career opportunity available with the company. Then, one day Geoff announced that he was to attend an interview for a job near his home in St Leonards-on-Sea. The interview was successful and Geoff tendered his resignation. The exciting prospect was a job with Peter Berthon, Raymond Mays' associate, and famous as the former designer of ERA and BRM racing cars. It was to be based at Berthon's home in Rye. The good news for me was that soon after Geoff left, news came that another designer was needed.

I duly attended for interview at The Roundel, Military Road,

in Rye. It was a far cry from AMC, as we would be working at two drawing boards set up in Peter's personal ground floor study, in the sumptuous and very personal surroundings of his home. The walls were covered with evocative pictures of BRMs, and outside the window was a pond with ducks and geese. A more striking contrast with the bustle of Woolwich could not have been found, and I couldn't wait to start.

When I had handed in my notice, Bill Martin, the Works Progress Manager, stopped me in the factory to express how sorry he was that I was leaving, and to ask about my plans. His response to my answer was to shake his head and say: "I would rather be a small fish in a big puddle than a big one in a small puddle. Small puddles can dry up quickly." It was a sobering thought, but, in the event, neither of us knew that both puddles were about to disappear more quickly than we expected, and at about the same time!

I left AMC at the end of March 1966 and started with Peter Berthon & Co on Monday 6th April. Regrettably, my unease with the situation proved right and, with an overdraft of £1.25 million, Barclays Bank appointed a receiver to manage the company's affairs early in August of the same year. The Plumstead business was sold to Manganese Bronze, and a new company, Norton Villiers, was formed. The AJS and Matchless ranges were now phased out in favour of the new and successful Norton Commando. My younger brother, Bob, five years my junior, had followed me in an apprenticeship with AMC, and was a significant player in this effective design team, staying with the company until the bitter end and the closure of motorcycle production at Plumstead in 1969. Motorcycles had been made there since the 1890s when H H Collier had his cycle business at 18 Herbert Road.

The basic plan at Peter Berthon & Co was to sell Peter's design expertise to the motor industry, with Geoff and I making the drawings under his guidance. In the event, the main project

NORTON VILLIERS LIMITED

NORTON MATCHLESS DIVISION
44 PLUMSTEAD ROAD, LONDON SE18
TELEPHONE 01-854 1223 TELEX 22617
CABLES NORTONMATCH LONDON TELEX

JP/EF/5.   18th June, 1969.

Dear *Mr. Jones*,

Thank you for your offer to continue your service with the
Company until the 23rd December, to assist with the initial
stages of production at Andover.

The period of extended service will be at your weekly wage of
the redundancy reference period, and your ultimate redundancy
entitlement will be no less favourable than if you had left on
the 25th July.

Your accommodation will be selected and paid for by the
Company, as will any travelling expenses incurred during your
service at Andover, and we know that you will do all in your
power to help during the period of your extended service.

Although you will be leaving the Company on the 23rd December,
your Christmas holiday entitlements will be honoured.

Yours sincerely,

JOHN REDLEY.
Director and General Manager,
Engine Division.

The final letter regarding termination of employment
addressed to tester Alan Jones. (Courtesy A Jones)

PETER BERTHON & CO. LTD.

P. L. A. Berthon   TELEPHONE RYE 3280   A. A. Berthon

ROUNDEL,
MILITARY ROAD,
RYE, SUSSEX

Your Ref.   Our Ref. PB/ZBGP/PBC   Date 22nd March,
                                                      1966.

W.A. Cakebread Esq.,
4, Braxfield Road,
Brockley,
LONDON, S.E.4.

Dear Mr. Cakebread,

Thank you for your letter of the 6th. I am glad to hear
that you will be able to start with us on Monday April 4th.

Dealing with the third paragraph of your letter, your
starting salary will be £20. 10. 0. per week, which figure
will be confirmed in any enquiries for property mortgage etc.

Yours sincerely,

Peter Berthon.

The offer letter from Peter Berthon.

Bob may design motor-cycles of the future

TWENTY-ONE-YEAR-OLD Robert Cakebread knows
a thing or two about motor-cycles—enough to make
him this year's top apprentice at Plumstead's Norton
Villiers firm.

Robert, of Colyers-close,
Northumberland Heath, received
his award at the Plumstead-road
factory last week. He is one of
12 apprentices training with
the new-style firm which is now
enjoying a big export boost.

Apprentices are judged on
their workmanship, general con-
duct and enthusiasm for work.
The foreman is asked for a
straight opinion too.

Robert said: "I suppose motorcycle careers run in the family.
My brother used to work at this
firm and my father is a keen
combination rider."

Robert sees motor-cycling's
future as good. He has been
working in the drawing office
for the past year and started his
apprenticeship at 16.

AMBITION

Now "Bob the Bike" hopes to
concentrate on motor cycle
design. He said: "I hope for
bigger things in that field later
on."

Other local budding appren-
tices this year included: Alan
Puplett, aged 19, of Altash-way,
Eltham and Christopher Grace,
also 19, of Whyncham-avenue,
Sidcup.

A Norton Villiers spokesman
said later: "We hope to take on
six more apprentices next year
and get the scheme really under
way."

On show at the award pre-
sentation—made by Mr. J. W.
Neville, vice-chairman of Norton
Villiers—was the new Com-
mando 750 machine which will
be on the market in the Spring.

Young Norton Villiers apprentices and one of Britain's top motor-cycles. Annual award
in the firm's apprenticeship scheme were presented at the Plumstead-road factory, Woolwich
last week. Left to right: Michael Bonner, John Foster, Chris Grace, Leslie Apps and Robert
Cakebread, the 21-year-old "top" apprentice of Erith.—(K.T. Photo No. K/7684B.

Press cutting. The Commando design team: my brother,
Bob, is on the far right.

was to design a four-valve V12 double overhead cam racing
engine for Ford, based on an existing and rather clumsy 3-valve
design that had been drawn. We were left mostly to our own
devices, and Peter's greatest assistance was in the form of a
file of drawings of the previous BRM engines for us to develop
ideas from. Nevertheless, it was very pleasurable. There were
four of us in total, Peter, Geoff, myself, and Peter's secretary, a
charming girl of Dutch descent with the unforgettable initials of
ZBGP (Zilla Beatrix Geraldine Persoon)! Peter's wife, Anthea,
and their two small children would visit occasionally to add a
little colour to the working day. Sometimes these distractions
(like the day when one of the geese attacked and tried to drown
one of the children in the pond), would get a little out of hand!

All of this comfort came to an end when Peter bought
Tollgate Garage on the corner of the Rye Harbour road. It was
an old-fashioned village garage when purchased, but with
a new forecourt installed by Jet, it became presentable and
appeared to have scope for the development that Peter intended.
A bungalow that stood on the corner of the plot was converted
into offices for Peter and Zilla and a Drawing Office for Geoff

and me. As in any small business, you become involved in everything and in this case that meant moving ourselves using an old, long-wheelbase open Land-Rover, one of the most pathetic vehicles that I have ever driven, and at least a close contender for that honour with the side-valve Morris Minor.

Work was still fun, with plenty of amusement and drama, as desperate attempts to build the business were made. We tried to secure agencies for Ford and Lotus without success. On one occasion, a Ford Cortina sale had been secured, but one in the right colour could not be sourced. As the staff in the workshop had little to do at the time, the new car was stripped to the bare shell, re-sprayed and re-assembled! On another memorable day, a transporter delivered a new Lotus Elan. A junior mechanic unloaded it and just couldn't resist giving it a quick blast down the road to Rye Harbour. Zonk! Unfortunately, there was no oil in the engine! I can't remember if Lotus ever accepted any responsibility, or if the mechanic's employment survived the incident.

Lunchtimes were particularly pleasant. Geoff and I would use our cars (Geoff a VW Beetle, me the MG ZA Magnette-LJB 100), on alternate days for our commute from St Leonards to Rye, picking up Zilla at Broad Oak, Brede, en route. At lunchtime, we would all pile into the car again and take our sandwiches down to the harbour where, summer and winter, we would watch the boating activity. These visits reinforced my love of the sea and ships and rekindled a long felt ambition to be part of it all.

Having successfully completed the V12 exercise, a single-cylinder prototype was built and tested by Ford. The feedback received reported a very narrow power band and a very high rotational speed to get it started! Nothing more was heard of it. Peter's plans to emulate his previous employer, Weslake, were clearly not coming to fruition, and no new projects were in the pipeline. Eventually, it was announced that our side of the business was to close, and Peter kindly organized interviews for us to secure continued employment at Ford.

For me, however, Ford and Dagenham was too closely associated with London. I had become used to breathing fresh air, enjoyed living by the sea, and had learned to sail a boat at the Hastings Sailing Club. (Incidentally, one of the stars of the Hastings Sailing Club at the time, sailing an International 5-0-5 with his brother, was former Matchless G45 racer Derek Farrant). I vowed not to return to city life. The motor industry had now twice kicked me in the teeth, and I decided that I would stay by the sea and find whatever employment I could. From now on, motor vehicles would be a hobby rather than a career. That was the plan, but it was not to remain that way for long and I never did fully escape my passion for vehicle engineering. Shortly after leaving Peter Berthon & Co., Peter sadly died in a swimming accident while on holiday.

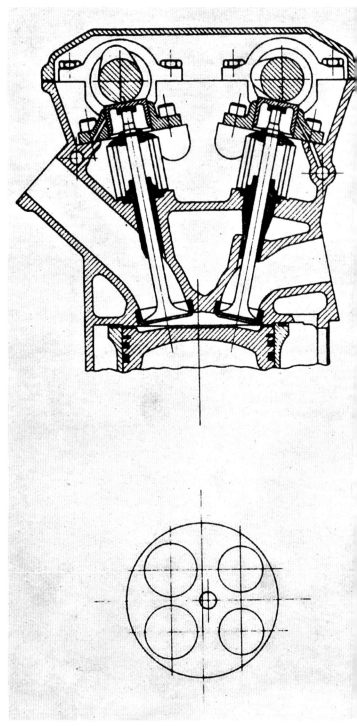

General arrangement of the proposed V12 cylinder head design.

21 AMC afterlife (cranes also have wheels)

The events outlined in the previous chapter brought to a close my immediate association with the motor industry for a while, unless you count the 33 years with Wylie whose business was associated with crane safety. Cranes generally have wheels or crawlers, so the association with vehicles was only truly lost for one year of my working life. The difference was that in this instance, instead of trying to make the vehicles go faster, the object was to try to stop them from falling over!

The passion for vehicles did not diminish in any way, however, and was satisfied by a whole variety of different cars and motorcycles. With a young family and a large mortgage to support, the vehicles that I purchased were not always in the best of condition, or the most desirable. Each, however, provided its own measure of enjoyment and education that helps to refine your taste in selecting what is best. The humble Mini-van (UDY 438) was notable for its economy, reliability, and usefulness, for instance, as was the comparative luxury of another MG ZB Magnette (UUC 923). This one had been found in a dealer's showroom. It was truly immaculate in black, but its price was a little more than I could afford. The dealer said that it was that price because the dynamo didn't work and the clutch needed to be replaced before he could sell it. I went back several times to look at it, and finally persuaded the dealer to sell it to me as it stood at a price that I could afford. On the strict understanding with the dealer that I might not get it home, I drove my prize away. The dynamo was easily cured by cleaning the commutator and freeing the brushes, and the car was enjoyed for many years. I did thousands of miles in that car and never did need to do anything to the clutch!

A Jaguar 420 provided yet more luxury, but the rate of movement on the fuel gauge was a depressing distraction from the enjoyment. At the other end of the scale, an Elva Courier, bought with a hardtop and tonneau, but with no hood, provided a great deal of fun. I used all of my vehicles for work, and the hardtop on the Elva was never used in the summer. One memorable moment involved a sudden thunderstorm, whilst I sat waiting at traffic lights, dressed in a business suit and tie, while water filled my lap (to the amusement of the surrounding motorists). A sporty-looking Morgan 4/4 with a side-valve Ford engine provided the most pathetic and embarrassing sports car motoring that I have ever endured. It looked good when it was parked, though!

Motorcycles are something that I can't live without, no matter how impractical the circumstances might be. When times were at their hardest, when my son was born, I owned a 1947 Scott Flying Squirrel, a rigid framed model with Dowty forks. The needs of my son came first, of course, and it was sold to finance the purchase of our first refrigerator. Many years later, when my son was taking a serious interest in motorcycles, he found a box of old photographs, including one of the Scott. He was very impressed by it, and asked me what it was and why I had sold it. When I explained that it was sold to buy a refrigerator so that his milk could be kept cool when he was a baby, he was distressed, and his reply was one that I will never forget; "Oh Dad, you should have kept it, I wouldn't have minded warm milk!"

After the demise of Peter Berthon & Co, the important task was to find employment, and I couldn't afford to be too choosy about what I did. To my surprise, however, I immediately found a position as a design draughtsman with W M Still in Hastings. This was a well established company, making boilers and associated equipment for the catering industry, and the factory in Hastings was quite modern. As a bonus, the pay was better, and it was closer to home, so my financial situation was improved at a stroke.

At first, everything seemed fine. The company treated its staff well and I soon became an accepted member of the design team. The design work, however, was so simplistic that there was no challenge or opportunity to use the skills that I had

Motorcycle Apprentice

learned. The Drawing Office Manager had been a faithful servant of the company for many years but, unfortunately, the drawing systems and control had not kept pace with the growth of the company. A clash with my professional motor industry training was inevitable. Quite a large proportion of the work was in the manufacture of stainless steel worktops and ovens, etc., and after a site survey, drawings would be prepared for the works to follow. The manager would generate crude sketches of what was required and expect the draughtsman to turn these into respectable drawings. He would insist that these were done on A4 plain paper which would then be photocopied. We were expected to just act as his 'pencils' and to have little input of our own. I found the work degrading after recently having proved my ability to draw and dimension most of the complex components to make a double-overhead camshaft twin! An example of the manager's way of thinking was illustrated to me when I followed him back to the factory after lunch one day. He was driving a small Ford saloon, while I was in the Mini-van. When we reached the right turn junction that led to the factory, he turned without signalling. Thinking that I was being helpful, when we had parked, I walked over to let him know that his right turn indicator was not working. His gruff reply surprised me; "Yes it is. I knew that it was you behind me so what was the point in wasting my indicators!" He was a good enough man, but I felt that the company needed more professionalism if it was to survive.

Eventually my abilities enabled me to gain a small 'promotion' by being given authority over my immediate associates in the Drawing Office, but the reward for the additional work and responsibility was not forthcoming. I finally put the case for my increased contribution and responsibilities to be recognized to the Technical Director but it was rejected. A few weeks later, when I finally tendered my notice, the reward that I had been requesting for months was suddenly made available, but it was too late. I was not prepared to play games.

The move to Wylie Safe Load Indicators Ltd was a risky step to take, and the start was not a promising one. I had replied to a newspaper advertisement for the position advertised under a box number, but had received no reply. Furious that this unknown company had my personal details and CV, I was surprised to see the same advertisement repeated a few weeks later. On this occasion, it was under the company name. The wording was identical and had obviously been written by the same person. I was livid at the discourtesy.

It is worth explaining that by this time, the burden of a large mortgage and the birth of my son were putting a severe strain on the finances. As a result of this and the generally lower standards that were accepted at W M Still, my dress code had relaxed into wearing a donkey jacket and slacks for work and my transport had been reduced to another, rather battered, green MG ZA (KPN 2) with torn seats purchased for £15 from a friend. Frustrated by desire for more professional employment, it was in this mode of dress and transport that I visited the offices of the company in question on my way home from work one evening. I had made no prior appointment.

I asked to see the Managing Director and, when requested by his secretary to say what it was about, I simply said "A complaint!" To my surprise, the gracious owner/Managing Director, Mr R L Aitken, agreed to see me and I immediately

A Boughton recovery crane. My interest in vehicle engineering was kept alive by working on vehicles like this.

The Coles 315M bridge-building crane.

launched into my anger at the lack of response to my job application. When I had calmed down a little, he apologized and enquired about my experience. He asked if I would like to see the factory. Then he posed the embarrassing question. His immaculate DB 4 Aston Martin (RLA 600) was being serviced, and the factory was half a mile away from the office. Could I take him in my car? To his eternal credit, he ignored the dents and the torn seats, and only commented on the qualities of the MG, which he compared with the Sunbeam Talbot that he had owned before the Aston. The work looked fascinating and very technical. I was keen, but he had a highly qualified design department. Could I survive in this environment?

Eventually he did offer me a position but only at exactly my current salary. Regrettably, I decided that it would be irresponsible to leave my secure and easy position at W M Still

for a job that I might not be able to handle. I telephoned from a callbox (I had not yet aspired to owning a telephone) to decline but before I could speak, he interrupted me to say that he had made a mistake about my age and the salary was actually 50p per week more than he had quoted. On that slender difference, I changed my mind, took the risk and accepted. I replaced the phone on its hook and decided that I must be mad!

As expected, I now faced a real challenge, as I was very much the junior in this office. They were a good and congenial crowd but at first I was in awe of their better qualifications. My design training and experience was sound, however, and my confidence was restored as I realized that I could hold my own with them on the drawing board. There were about six or seven design draughtsmen, plus a Technical Director and Chief Engineer who shared a separate office. The company had recently

Motorcycle Apprentice

re-located its design and prototype manufacturing facilities to Hastings from Bow in East London, so the facilities were modern and comfortable. The exciting thing in this company, in marked contrast with anything that I had known before, was the rate of development and the vast amount of new 'clean sheet' design work that was undertaken. Even in my beloved motor industry, true development of entirely new designs was extremely rare, and changes to existing designs were made at a relatively slow pace. In this office, an idea alone could quickly turn into a prototype of a new product within weeks. It was daunting but exciting and exactly the challenge that my brain had been looking for.

Although the work was interesting, the office itself was not a particularly industrious one, and we were a fairly laid back bunch of diverse characters. The fact that the Managing Director's office was located half a mile away did not help. The Technical Director was frequently called to attend meetings there, and when he was away, the work rate noticeably slowed. Even when he was there, the laid back attitude persisted, and he would often initiate an unofficial break himself by purchasing ice-creams for us whenever an ice-cream van was around. The work arrangement was that each of us would be set to work on our own design project. The progress and direction of these was overseen by the Technical Director with occasional visits by the owner, Mr Aitken, to comment or make some radical off-the-wall change in direction. A quite amazing Victorian feature of these visits was that Mr Aitken insisted that we all wore white coats and addressed each other only by our surnames when in his company. Christian names were definitely not permitted. It was weird.

In spite of my lowly qualifications, ambition still drove me to want to achieve more, and I had a pride in design work that seemed to be lacking in some of my colleagues. Some were undoubtedly better draughtsmen than me, but they did not seem to possess the desire to design creatively. Then the Technical Director returned one day from one of his meetings with 'the old man' with the news that there was a need for an entirely new product development. The requirement had been outlined but they had decided in their wisdom that we were all too busy; definitely not the case. Also, the requirement was complex with no obvious solution. They had, therefore, decided to sub-contract the project to a professional design centre in London.

It was a typical reaction in the office that this was just one less job that we had to do, but I was incensed! The design ability of our office had been insulted, and we'd been given no opportunity to show what we could achieve. Who did they think they were to imagine that some high-priced London design consultancy was more capable than we were? The Technical Director left shortly after making the announcement to return to yet another meeting, while the office relaxed back into its normal ponderous routine. I was not satisfied with this at all and replaced the current design project on my drawing board with a clean sheet of paper. I started to sketch and, by going home time that same day, I had completed a scheme of what I thought would be a working solution. Before I left, I rolled it up and left it on the Technical Director's desk without explanation. When I arrived the next morning, questions were asked. The

London sub-contractors were cancelled, and my design was put into production. The junior guy with the lowly qualifications had been noticed!

In retrospect, there followed an embarrassing exercise which none of us in the office saw coming. After the aforementioned project, the management decided to make a logical change to our system of work. Instead of each of us slowly developing our own projects, and making the detailed drawings of it, one project at a time would be selected for priority completion. The others would then produce the detail drawings for that project leader. It just so happened that the project that I was working on was selected as the first priority. To their credit, everyone pitched in willingly and submitted to my direction of the design. On completion, I was promoted to Drawing Office Manager! I was sincerely embarrassed, as it now became clear that the management, naturally lacking confidence that this newcomer could lead this highly qualified team, had set this up as a test for me. After little more than a year I found myself in charge of all of the people that I had previously been in awe of. It was a big step and a daunting one.

Following that improbable start, I progressed through the consecutive positions from Design Engineer to Drawing Office Manager within the space of a year, and then to Engineering Manager, Sub-Contracts Manager, Sales Manager, Sales Director, Marketing Director, and finally to Managing Director and a Director of the Rayco Technology Group in Canada, which, by then, had become the new owner of the company.

The work, particularly in engineering and sales, involved much contact with the crane manufacturers and, once again, I was working on vehicles on a production line. It was always a joy to be around the manufacture of new vehicles with the sights and smells of fresh oil and new tyres. Dirty secondhand vehicles are not the same and I was never inclined to work in a service environment. This company also introduced me to travelling the world and dealing with different cultures, an educating experience for which I will also be eternally grateful.

It's strange how fate can take a hand just when all seems to be going so well, and this was where the problems started with the company. The move from engineering to sales had been initiated by me because I could see no path for further career advancement on the engineering side. The Technical Director above me was too young, and sales were at a low ebb at the time. I gladly accepted the challenge (and my first company car!) and set myself a large personal target. A major military contract for bridge-building cranes was out for tender and it was generally accepted that one of our major competitors would be awarded the contract to supply the safety instrumentation. The contract was already at an advanced stage and I spent a disproportionate amount of time and effort in trying to reverse this expected conclusion. At one stage, the Managing Director called me into the office to reprimand me and instructed that I should not be wasting my time. He changed his mind when we won the contract; "We always knew that you would do it my boy!"

It was the biggest single contract that the company had ever secured, but disaster was waiting in the wings. When we were in full production with an excess of unpaid for stock on

The last project before retirement — arriving in the Spa 24 hour race-winning Aston Martin at Brooklands in 2006. (Courtesy Tim Cottingham — AMOC)

the customer's premises, the apparently prosperous client went out of business! What we had not seen was that the group that owned the company, with which we had no direct dealings, was in financial difficulties and had called in some inter-company debts. Our customer went bust and we suffered horrendous losses. How quickly success can turn to failure. From that point onward, our previously cash-rich company was forced to borrow, and found difficulty in servicing the loans. An exercise with a venture capital group diluted the family shareholding and only seemed to make matters worse until eventually the family ownership of the company was lost. The company was sold to a Canadian company, The Rayco Technology Group. Although I became Managing Director of the UK operation following the takeover, the next few years were dispiriting as the UK input diminished and the technology base moved to Canada. After 33 years, we mutually agreed to a parting of the ways. Walking out of that door for the last time was one of the most emotional and difficult things that I have done in my career, second only to leaving AMC.

One door closes and another one opens! At 59 years of age, my employment prospects did not look good and so I set up a small consultancy business offering my services in crane safety training and general management, but it was only a matter of months before one of my clients offered me a directorship to help manage his company. It was back in the motor trade and I was at home again!

The company, Constables Ltd, was manufacturing and converting vehicles for the disabled, but fresh direction was sorely needed. It was not difficult and I immediately felt at home in the place. The production figures rose, quality standards were raised, staff motivation and rewards improved, and profits hit an all time high. For four years I was left very much alone to do my job, and thoroughly enjoyed myself. Unfortunately, this happy situation was not set to last forever. In June 2004, I was fortunate enough to have acquired a very rare Aston Martin at auction that required total restoration. It had a fascinating history and had won the Spa 24 hour race outright in 1948. It seemed that it would be well worth the effort and so, with two years left to my official retirement date, I decided to devote my time to that project rather than face the daily aggravation of my employment. It was the right decision to take and so my career ended still working with the motor vehicles that I loved. The wheel had turned full circle and I was now working with my hands again, just as I did at the start of my apprenticeship.

The point in including this information post-AMC is that, quite often in my career, I've been fortunate to hold quite senior positions of authority. I don't count myself as being clever, nor were any of my modest achievements particularly worthy of note. That I was able to achieve anything at all, other than the most menial of employment, however, is entirely due to the practical training and experience that was gained during my apprenticeship with AMC. Building on that, of course, thanks is

Motorcycle Apprentice

due to the individuals who, later in my career, were brave enough to put their faith in me, a faith which they could not justify by paperwork qualifications alone.

To Associated Motor Cycles Ltd, and to those individuals, I offer my eternal gratitude. The AMC apprenticeship had truly been 'Matchless-in name and reputation,' just like it said on the packaging for the products!

Guaranteed to be 'Matchless'!

Visit Veloce on the web — www.veloce.co.uk
Details of all books in print • Special offers • New book news • Gift vouchers

110

22 Homecoming

Mr P. McGreevy, Director of Leisure Services
has pleasure in inviting you to the opening of

MADE IN  PLUMSTEAD

To be opened by Mr P. Bottomley M.P., Under-Secretary of State,
Department of Transport

16th February
6.30–8.30pm

Greenwich Borough Museum
232 Plumstead High Street
London SE18 1JT

Evening invitation.

Twenty years after production at the Plumstead factory finally ceased, in 1989 Greenwich Borough Museum organized 'The AMC Homecoming Rally.' The factory had long since been demolished following removal of the final production run of Nortons, and the remaining staff moved to Andover in the summer of 1969. Two events were organized. The first, on 16th February, was an evening meeting at the museum; essentially a reunion of former employees, but the organizers arranged an excellent display of memorabilia in honour of the company's past glory. On 14th May, this was followed by a gathering of machines, ex-employees, and the AJS and Matchless Owners Club at a convivial meeting in Beresford Square, Woolwich.

My wife and I attended on a 1957 International Norton. The sun shone and the atmosphere was good as long-lost former associates slowly recognized one another. In addition to changes in our physical appearances, however, there was no escaping the fact that time had moved on. Apart from the absence of the factory, the Arsenal itself was strangely quiet, and Beresford Square seemed unfamiliar without its bustling market stalls. All around the main shopping street there was an atmosphere of decay, with only the smallest signs of re-generation evident. An era had ended.

At its peak, the company had produced 96 motorcycles in a day and had employed around 1500 people. The marking of its passing was sad, not just for the employees who had been so emotionally involved in it, or the motorcycle industry as a whole, but for the entire country.

Memories are revived at the evening reception.

Wheel builder 'Tiger' Smith and tester Alan Jones share reminiscences.

Homecoming Rally programme — front page.

The AMC Homecoming Rally, Beresford Square, Woolwich, 1989.

The end. The crumbling walls of the partly demolished factory. The back page of the 'Homecoming' programme says it all.

23 (Just) another plaque on the wall

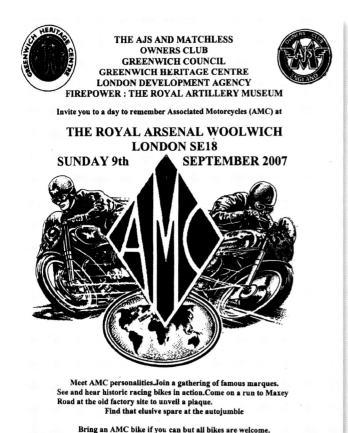

THE AJS AND MATCHLESS
OWNERS CLUB
GREENWICH COUNCIL
GREENWICH HERITAGE CENTRE
LONDON DEVELOPMENT AGENCY
FIREPOWER : THE ROYAL ARTILLERY MUSEUM

Invite you to a day to remember Associated Motorcycles (AMC) at

THE ROYAL ARSENAL WOOLWICH
LONDON SE18
SUNDAY 9th   SEPTEMBER 2007

Meet AMC personalities. Join a gathering of famous marques.
See and hear historic racing bikes in action. Come on a run to Maxey
Road at the old factory site to unveil a plaque.
Find that elusive spare at the autojumble

Bring an AMC bike if you can but all bikes are welcome.
Follow signs to FIREPOWER. The event starts at 10.00 and it's free!

LONDON
DEVELOPMENT
AGENCY

Greenwich
Council

FIREPOWER
THE ROYAL ARTILLERY MUSEUM

Advertising flyer for the 2007 meeting.

On 9th September 2007, another reunion meeting was organized by the Greenwich Heritage Centre in conjunction with the AJS and Matchless Owners Club. On this occasion, the venue was within the Woolwich Arsenal itself.

Both the Arsenal and the surrounding area were barely recognizable. Most of the massive Arsenal production buildings had gone and, in their place, was a very tasteful riverside development containing new housing and a military museum complex. Within the Arsenal walls, the atmosphere was serene and very peaceful. It was as if the bustle of London just outside the walls did not exist. It was an ideal venue for a perfect day.

Outside, it was a different story and it was difficult at first to recognize where the factory had once stood. The previous single carriageway Plumstead Road was now a dual carriageway with two lanes heading east and another two plus a bus lane heading west towards the Woolwich Ferry. To confuse matters further, the massive continuous wall that previously surrounded the Arsenal had been demolished and replaced by another boundary to make room for the wider road. The new road now passes inside where the Arsenal wall once was! Incongruously, this leaves the impressive and preserved entrance gate building isolated on an island of its own in Beresford Square, with the new road now running behind it.

Getting one's bearings at the old factory site was also more difficult than had been imagined. Some major landmark buildings like public houses had gone, and, apart from some surviving road names, the only features that were immediately recognizable were the railway bridges in Maxey and Burrage Roads, and the old school building adjacent to the factory. The whole area where the factory formerly stood is now a housing estate, and some of the new buildings have been built across Burrage Grove. This road previously separated the main factory from the Race and Repair Shops, and had once been the scene of so much activity. The occupants of the new properties were

115

Burrage Grove as it is today. The houses are built across the road where the factory once stood.

A similar view taken during a typical London 'smog' in 1956. The wire fence is roughly where the houses now stand. (Courtesy P Stevens)

Some of the original assembly shop testers added to the occasion. Still riding, of course, are Alan Jones, Cyril Ford and Bill Hawkins.

going about their daily business of shopping and cleaning their cars, etc., and I couldn't help but wonder if any of them had any awareness of the history beneath their feet. Did anyone ever sense the hum of the machine shops in the dead of the night, or feel the vibrations from a racing engine on full bore from the subterranean test beds that once lived beneath their floors? I'm sure that they would be blissfully unaware, but for me, at least, the ghosts were very real.

The focal point of the meeting was to lay a plaque to mark the site where the factory had once stood, and the corner of Maxey and Plumstead Roads was chosen as the most appropriate and nearest location. The smart new flats that now occupy the hallowed ground are surrounded only by a low brick wall and it is on this wall that the plaque, somehow small and low to the ground relative to the former might of the company that it

records, is mounted. However small, we should be grateful that some attempt at least has been made to mark this site of our once proud industrial history.

The date chosen was said to have been selected to mark the 40th anniversary of the final finish of production, but many workers there remembered that manufacture of Norton Commandos at least, continued until the final closure of the factory in 1969. It would seem that there had been much effort made to agree with the authorities that the site should be marked over the years. Having finally reached agreement, it was apparently decided to 'seize the moment' and have the plaque sited before someone changed their mind! The date chosen would, therefore, appear to have been more political than historical, and I consoled myself with the thought that perhaps the last Matchless may have rolled off the production

There was a fine display of the quality racing machinery that the factory had produced.

line at around that time. The Collier family would have been happy with that.

If ever there was to be a meeting to mark the closure of the factory, then this one certainly did it justice. The setting was superb. A portion of the Royal Arsenal site and its surviving buildings was being tastefully preserved amongst the new housing development, and a wide central spine road running from the old Brass Foundry building to the river provided an ideal site to show off the bikes. This was beautifully paved and, together with the 'Firepower' museum's refreshment facilities, provided a most congenial atmosphere.

The sun also provided its blessing as literally hundreds of the factory's finest products arrived from all directions to park neatly down one side of the spine road. To my shame, at the time of the event we did not own a motorcycle of AMC manufacture, but the invitation in the motorcycle press made the statement that 'all makes are welcome.' We took them at their word and

arrived on a 1937 350cc Excelsior Manxman. Our embarrassment did not end there as, when we arrived and tried to park with the 'other makes,' an official of the AJS and Matchless Owners Club stopped us and directed us to an enclosure where there was a display of AMC competition machines. Apparently, they thought that the Manxman was too interesting to park anywhere else! At first I felt awkward to be an intruder in this fine display of AMC racing machinery, but then I spotted two lovely pre-war AJS overhead-cam racers in the display. They both had the right badge on their tanks, of course, but like the Excelsior, they looked too early to have a true connection with manufacture at the Plumstead factory.

The ceremony to unveil the plaque involved a ride by all the road legal bikes from the Arsenal to the Maxey Road location on a small circular tour of the area. The police were superb, and controlled every road junction so that our progress was not impeded. This area of London is quite busy, but at the site the

Another plaque on the wall

police had closed the bus lane to provide parking for us. With the ceremony completed, they then also cleared the nearside lane to enable us to filter back into the traffic flow with safety! They did an excellent job and deserve our thanks.

Back at the Arsenal, the day just became better and better as the rarest of AMC racing machinery was brought to life for 'demonstration' runs down the spine road. The stars were the pre-war V4 AJS and the AJS Porcupine running in its later un-supercharged specification. These were supported by a batch of AJS 7Rs, Matchless G50s and Seeleys, with Colin Seeley himself riding his own creations. Colin had purchased the AMC Race Shop when the factory closed, and successfully continued the development of the racing bikes, employing my brother Bob, and another ex-apprentice Les Apps, in the process. Sometimes the bikes ran in batches of three so that the spectacle was more like a sprint or drag race than a demonstration run. I don't know if all this activity was planned or was impromptu but, however it happened, the sight and sounds of that wonderful machinery made a good day perfect and truly memorable. There may be other reunions in the future, but on this day, with the laying of the plaque, I felt that the old factory had truly been laid to rest. I like to think that the Collier brothers would have approved.

It was not just a static display! Here, Sammy Miller rides the rare water-cooled V4 in the demonstration.

Behind this wall lies the site of the Associated Motorcycles factory where Matchless, AJS, Norton and other marques were manufactured until 1967.

This plaque was erected to commemorate the 40th anniversary of the end of motorcycle production in Woolwich. It was unveiled by Councillor Peter Brooks, Deputy Leader of Greenwich Council, on Sunday 9 September 2007.

The plaque is the only record that remains to mark the site of this once proud factory. (Courtesy R A Cakebread)

24 Management (a comment)

When I first joined AMC as a naïve apprentice, I had a simplistic vision of management. My parents had brought me up to work hard, to respect authority, and to be loyal above all else.

I, therefore, assumed that if I did all of these things for my employer, I would in return be rewarded by his loyalty, and that my security would be assured. As I worked my way up through the various strata of management, however, it became apparent (with a few notable exceptions) that self-interest increasingly became the focus for many of my peers. They seemed to have a progressively diminishing regard for the consequences of their actions on the employees below them, as their own careers and wealth advanced.

At the uppermost levels of company management/ownership, I found also the highest levels of self-interest, corruption and dishonesty. It was a disappointment.

It is also shattering to remember those first weeks of my apprenticeship in the Drilling Shop, and to think that the actions of one thoughtless chargehand came so close to breaking my spirit and making me leave. With no qualifications to my name, his actions could have changed the course of my life completely and cost me my career. It is a sobering thought.

The enthusiasm remains ...

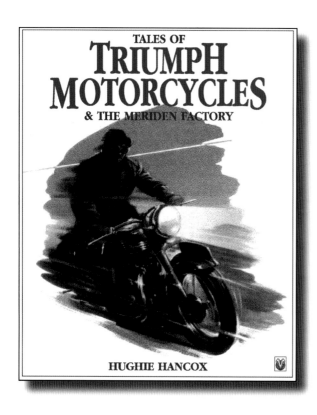

Tales of Triumph Motorcycles & the Meriden Factory

Hughie Hancox • Paperback • 25x20.7cm • £12.99*
• 144 pages • 91 b&w pictures
ISBN 978-1-901295-67-2

Hughie worked at Triumph from 1954 until its closure in 1974. Here's the story of his life in the famous Meriden factory; of many adventures with Triumph motorcycles & Triumph people. Records the fascinating history of a great marque.

Also from Veloce Publishing

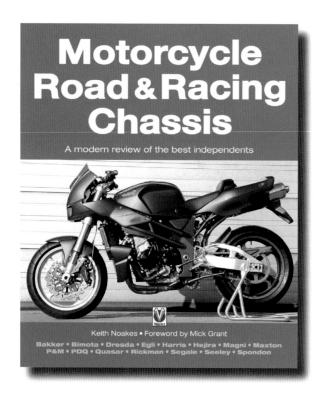

Motorcycle Road & Racing Chassis

Keith Noakes • Paperback • 250x207mm • £19.99*
• 176 pages • 246 mainly colour illustrations
ISBN 978-1-845841-30-0

An account of the independent companies and individuals who have played a major part in the design and advancement of motorcycle frame (chassis) performance. With full specifications for many chassis and extensively illustrated throughout, this book is a must for any motorcycle enthusiast and a valuable reference for the trade.

Triumph Speed Twin & Thunderbird Bible

Harry Woolridge • Hardback • 25x20.7cm • £25.00*
• 144 pages • 142 photos
ISBN 978-1-904788-263

The complete technical development history of the Triumph Speed Twin and Thunderbird motorcycles, and an invaluable reference source to identification, specification, exact year of manufacture and model type. A must for all Triumph lovers.

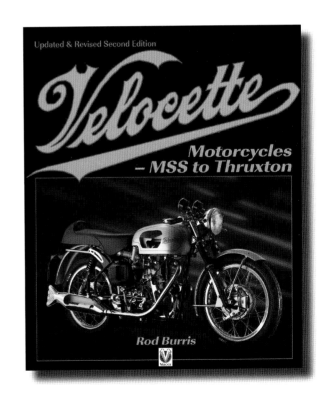

Velocette Motorcycles – MSS to Thruxton

Rod Burris • Hardback • 25x20.7cm • £29.99*
• 160 pages • 308 colour & b&w photos
ISBN 978-1-904788-28-7

The definitive development history of the most famous Velocette motorcycles, based on the author's earlier work, out of print for many years and much sought-after today. Includes the most comprehensive appendices ever published on this historic marque.

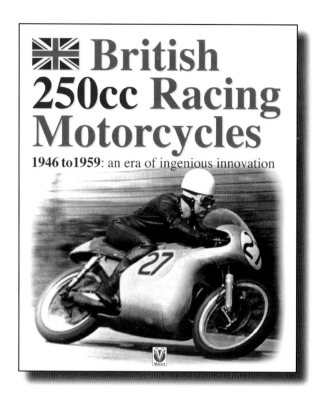

British 250cc Racing Motorcycles 1946-1959

Chris Pereira • Hardback • 25x20.7cm • £15.99*
• 80 pages • 97 monochrome photographs
ISBN 978-1-904788-12-6

The history and development of the privately-built, British 250cc specials and hybrids raced in Britain from 1946 to 1959, recalling the men and machines involved in what was clearly the most innovative class of road racing in the 1950s.

The Triumph Trophy Bible

Harry Woolridge • Hardback • 25x20.7cm • £30.00*
• 144 pages • Over 130 pictures
ISBN 978-1-904788-02-7

Complete year-by-year history of the Trophy (and unit construction Tiger) twins from 1949 to 1983. Includes original factory model photos, technical specifications, colour schemes, engine & frame numbers, model type identification and details of Trophy & Tiger achievements. The complete source book.

The Triumph Tiger Cub Bible

Mike Estall • Hardback • 25x20.7cm • £35.00*
• 208 pages • 210 b&w photographs
ISBN 978-1-904788-09-6

The full history of the popular Triumph Cub motorcycle. This ultimate reference source book covers every aspect of these machines, including 22 detailed model profiles, delivery details, technical design specifications, military, police and competition bikes, plus the full story behind the model's production run.

*All prices subject to change, p&p extra
www.veloce.co.uk, info@veloce.co.uk
Tel. +44 (0) 1305 260068

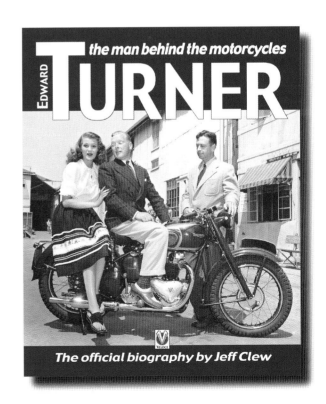

Edward Turner – The man behind the motorcycles

Jeff Clew • Paperback • 25x20.7cm • £17.99*
• 160 pages • 140 colour & b&w photos
ISBN 978-1-84584-065-5

"Turner was an inventive genius who had a flair for pleasing shapes and an uncanny ability to perceive what the buying public would readily accept, to produce it at the right price." For the first time the life of Edward Turner, one of Britain's most talented motorcycle designers, is revealed in full.

Index

Motorcycle Apprentice